Strip-Pieced Bargello

DYNAMIC QUILTS, STEP BY STEP

Judith Steele

Martingale
Create with Confidence

Strip-Pieced Bargello: Dynamic Quilts, Step by Step
© 2019 by Judith Steele

Martingale®
19021 120th Ave. NE, Ste. 102
Bothell, WA 98011-9511 USA
ShopMartingale.com

Printed in China
24 23 22 21 20 19   8 7 6 5 4 3 2 1

Library of Congress Cataloging-in-Publication Data is available upon request.

ISBN: 978-1-60468-986-0

MISSION STATEMENT

We empower makers who use fabric and yarn to make life more enjoyable.

CREDITS

PUBLISHER AND CHIEF VISIONARY OFFICER
Jennifer Erbe Keltner

CONTENT DIRECTOR
Karen Costello Soltys

MANAGING EDITOR
Tina Cook

ACQUISITIONS EDITOR
Amelia Johanson

TECHNICAL EDITOR
Nancy Mahoney

COPY EDITOR
Melissa Bryan

DESIGN MANAGER
Adrienne Smitke

COVER AND BOOK DESIGNER
Regina Girard

PHOTOGRAPHER
Brent Kane

ILLUSTRATOR
Christine Erikson

SPECIAL THANKS
Photography for this book was taken at the home of Jodi and Lance Allen in Woodinville, Washington.

DEDICATION

To the memory of my father, who was delighted with my achievements in the world of bargello quilts. He encouraged me to keep on designing and bought a copy of every magazine that published one of my designs for as long as he was able.

Contents

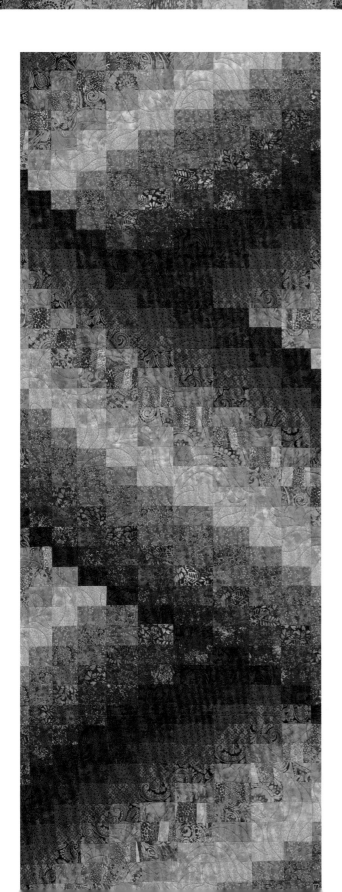

Quilt Gallery Online!

To see more bargello quilts and handy metric conversion tables, visit ShopMartingale.com/Strip-PiecedBargello.

Introduction

Having started my working life as a carpet designer, a discipline where single *pics* (tufts) of carpet yarn are combined to create a myriad of patterns, I was mesmerized the first time I saw a picture of a bargello quilt. It was called Lightning Strikes by Chris Timmins, and it appeared in an Australian patchwork magazine back in 2001.

I read the article about Chris, then read the instructions for making the quilt, and then—deciding that it sounded fairly straightforward—went ahead and started making a bargello quilt of my own. The tools I had on hand were Microsoft's software program Excel (which I still use today for designing quilts), scissors, iron and ironing board, seam ripper, and sewing machine. Having had no quilting lessons, I'd never heard of cutting mats, rotary cutters, or any of the other aids we seem to think are essential these days. So I cut all the strips using my scissors. The resulting quilt is still on my bed and serves as a reminder of all the things not to do when making a bargello quilt.

Throughout the process, I often thought that there must be a better way to measure and cut. The next time I attended a craft fair, I saw a Sew Easy Ruler Cutter, a combination gadget offering both measuring and cutting functions. I bought it immediately (before somebody else did) and I'm still using it today.

I also became interested in the origins of bargello designs and found they dated back to the 1300s. There are several legends explaining the birth of bargello, and the one I like best is that a Hungarian princess married a member of the de' Medici family, then proceeded to decorate her new home with the beautiful flame-patterned tapestries she had brought with her to the Bargello Palace in Florence. They became known as Florentine work and bargello embroidery designs.

Bargello embroidery appears to have remained the only bargello textile craft until the 1960s, when someone turned the tapestry designs into knitting patterns. Later in the 20th century, an inspired individual turned a bargello tapestry into a quilt design. The idea caught on and blossomed into the many bargello quilt designs and techniques available today.

Many quilters, from beginner to advanced, are intimidated by the seeming complexity of bargello designs. I had the benefit of already knowing, from my carpet-designing days, that it's possible to create curves using only straight lines. Following a pattern set out in a grid, as I did for my first bargello quilt, can turn the most complex pattern into a project that is easy to make. The biggest bonus is that it's all straight sewing.

In this book are tips and techniques for making the construction process easier. I'll explain which fabrics are ideal for bargello quilts and which fabrics should be avoided. I'll also cover the basic principles of bargello designs, following that up with a variety of projects using bargello strips and blocks. If you live in a part of the world that uses the metric system, you'll find conversion tables at ShopMartingale.com/Strip-PiecedBargello.

The book is not prescriptive; if you find other ways of doing things that suit you better, then go right ahead and do your own thing. I'm a notorious rule breaker, so how could I condemn anyone else for what I do myself? To me the main thing is to enjoy the process and experience the immense satisfaction of looking at a finished project and telling myself with a smile, "I made that!"

Fabric Choices

It's exciting when the time comes to choose fabrics for a new bargello project. There are some guidelines to bear in mind, but few hard-and-fast rules. The main one is never to buy a fabric you don't like—and if someone else gives you something hideous, re-gift it!

Most quilters use fabrics that are 100% cotton, but you can use any type of fabric that strikes your fancy. One guideline is to stick with the same type of fabric throughout a project so that, if the quilt is washed a lot, you won't face puckering or tearing caused by different rates of shrinkage in different parts of the quilt. Quilts created only for display are sometimes constructed of fabrics such as velvets, silks, and polyesters, and some are even made of paper, but these are the exceptions.

The realization of how many different fabrics you'll need for a project can be daunting. If you're not confident in choosing fabrics, ask for help from quilting friends or the staff at your local quilt shop. If you have your own fabric stash, that's a good place to start.

Color

Often, deciding what colors to use is the hardest choice you'll face when making a bargello project. Do you want to use just one segment of the color spectrum, or go wild and use a whole rainbow of colors? What you choose will depend on the look you want to achieve and also on the project you're planning to make. If you can't make up your mind, start with your favorite color or a color combination that you like.

Staying within one color family, while including one fabric that stands out from the others, is a good choice for a project that requires only a few fabrics.

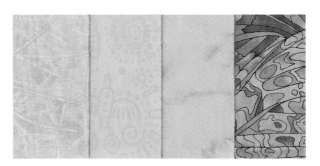

The darkest green used for the Diamond Star Tote on page 30 is distinctive, but still blends into the overall color scheme.

For a project with many fabrics, such as Dreamland's Curtain on page 15, choose a few fabrics from every color of the rainbow with a "standout" fabric in several color groups to add interest and definition to the finished quilt.

Standout Fabric

A standout fabric is one that appears a bit more prominent than those around it and adds an element of visual interest. It draws your eye first to the boundaries between it and the colors next to it, before your eye roams further to appreciate the other colors in the project.

In some cases, a project calls for colors from two color groups, such as the Autumn Leaves table runner on page 22. For that project, high contrast between the first and last colors in the color run prevents the design from fading into a mix of similar hues.

Usually you're trying to achieve a gradual change of color across the color run, an effect sometimes referred to as ombré, with a lot of contrast between the first and last colors. A color run is the sequence of colors in a color family, grading from light to dark or, less often, from dark to light. The steps in the sequence are usually a consistent amount darker along the color run, unless a standout fabric is used to add visual interest.

The contrast between the yellow and black fabrics in Autumn Leaves (page 22) elevates the visibility of the design.

Scale

Scale refers to the size of the patterned design on the fabric. In general, bargello quilts look better when made from plainer fabrics, such as solid colors, tone on tones, and small-scale prints. However, just as adding a standout color can add sparkle to a design, using one or two standout prints can mean the difference between an OK quilt and one you really love. This was the case with Stormy Seas on page 70. I wasn't entirely satisfied with my fabric choices until I included a light, large-scale floral printed on a dark background and noticed the interesting effect it created.

A large-scale floral adds the perfect dose of extra interest to the quilt Stormy Seas.

Standout fabrics play an important role in creating movement in bargello quilts, but don't get too carried away. To get a better idea of the overall effect of different fabrics in a color run, arrange the fabrics with each one showing the amount that will appear in a strip set. Then stand back or take a photo. If one fabric catches your eye and stops your gaze from roaming across the other colors, it's too conspicuous and needs to be replaced with something more subdued.

Another trap for the unwary is to use a lot of fabrics with small prints or similar patterns next to one another in the color run. When grouped together, similar-looking prints tend to lose definition and you'll find it hard to discern the bargello design. A tone-on-tone fabric or a plain color between busier prints can help prevent this problem.

Prints with large-scale patterns and a lot of colors can also ruin the look of your finished quilt, because there is no consistency of pattern or color across the patches of this fabric. A large part of the beauty of bargello designs depends on their regularity and sense of harmony. A striking large-scale print can still be a candidate, however, as long as it includes some of the colors around it and also contains one contrasting color that makes it suitable as a standout fabric. In that situation, the print can add marvelous interest and movement to the quilt.

A large-scale print in Riding the Waves, shown in full on page 47, contains colors that blend beautifully with those around it, as well as white, which adds contrast and interest.

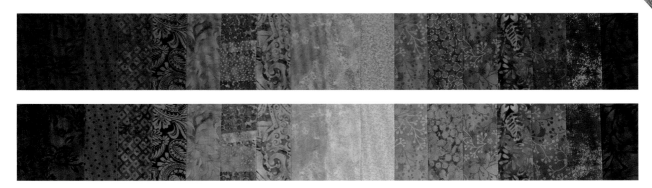

Comparing a color photo of the Down the Bannister color run to a black-and-white image clarifies the change in value from dark to light and then back to dark.

Value

In the context of patchwork and quilting, value doesn't refer to how much you paid for that gorgeous fabric, but rather, how light or dark a fabric is in relation to the other fabrics around it. In most bargello projects, you're instructed to find fabrics that range in value from light to dark or dark to light. In some cases this is fairly easy, but at other times it's very difficult to decide on the order in which fabrics should appear. To compound the issue, a fabric that appears dark in one color run can look medium or even light in a different context. Luckily, there are a couple of strategies to help you make these decisions.

The simplest way is to arrange the fabrics in an order that you think looks good, showing an equal amount of each fabric. Next take a photo, and then, using the readily available digital tools for photo effects, change the photo to black and white (or, if possible, simply take a black-and-white photo). Instantly, you'll be able to see the dark and light values of the fabrics.

You may choose to leave the fabrics in the original order, or rearrange them to more closely follow their values. But always remember, *color trumps value every time!* Looking at the color run for Stormy Seas (page 70) in black and white reveals that fabric 9 is darker in value than fabrics 10 and 11. The reason I left it there is because it's an aqua color and better matches the other aqua fabrics, while colors 10 and 11 are much greener. Don't fall into the trap of arranging your fabrics only by value, as your color run may not actually run from one shade to the next but have quite different colors mixed together.

Another method of determining the optimal fabric order is by using a tool called a value finder, such as the Ruby Beholder. This is a piece of red colored plastic you hold up to your eye to view your fabrics. A green version is also available for viewing red-based fabrics. Both versions mask the fabric colors, allowing you to see only the value of the fabric.

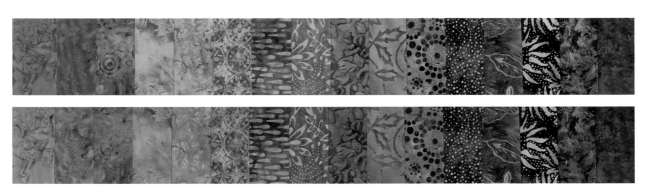

Comparing a color photo of the Stormy Seas color run to a black-and-white image reveals that, for this quilt, color has been given more importance than value.

Strip Sets and Blocks

Bargello quilts are made from strips of different fabrics, usually cut to the same width, which are sewn into strip sets (sometimes called strata). The strip sets are then crosscut into segments of varying widths. The segments are offset to create a stair-step effect of like fabrics. Then the segments are stitched together to make the quilt top. In many bargello patterns, some seams on a segment are removed to make partial segments, which are then used to form the design. The variation in the width of the segments creates an optical illusion of curves that appear to bend and turn up, down, and across the design. Most of the projects in this book are made in this manner.

In bargello blocks, different fabrics are likewise cut into strips of varying widths before being sewn into strip sets. The strip sets are crosscut into strips of varying widths before being sewn into blocks, with the colors offset by one position each. Bargello blocks can create an optical illusion that looks like a quarter circle, and the blocks can be arranged in hundreds of different ways to create interesting and beautiful patterns. Dancing Butterflies on page 63 is made this way and represents just one of the many possible block arrangements.

Preparing a Fabric Guide

Whether preparing to make a bargello project with strips or with blocks, the first step is to decide on the specific fabrics you'll use. Most bargello patterns suggest a color combination ranging from light to dark (or dark to light) in one or two color groups, although there are exceptions. For some people, putting the fabrics into the "right" order can take longer than making the project. The right order is a color combination and sequence that *you* like, bearing in mind the guidelines and suggestions in "Fabric Choices" on page 5 and the destination of the finished piece. Choosing fabrics and placing them in the right order takes a bit of practice, but it gets easier over time.

Once you've settled on the order of your colors, cut a small piece from each of the fabrics. Glue the swatches onto a piece of paper or thin cardboard in the order they will appear in the project. Then write the fabric number alongside each fabric. This will be your fabric guide. The fabric guide shows the numerical order of the fabrics and should be displayed prominently near your sewing machine. Having a visual aid is very important, as it's easy to get fabrics of similar colors in the wrong order when making the strip sets.

Fabric guide for Riding the Waves on page 46.
Fabrics are numbered from lightest to darkest, 1–18.

Preparing Fabrics

There's considerable disagreement among quilters about whether or not to prewash fabrics and how to do it. As most of the quilted items we make are intended for everyday use, I think it's advisable to prewash all of your fabrics to take care of any shrinkage and color running that may occur.

I always wash similar colors together in hot water, using two or three color-catcher sheets in each wash. This way the fabrics will shrink, if they're going to, and will release any excess dye that the color-catcher sheets pick up from the water. Darker colors usually release more dye than lighter colors. Washing also removes any remaining sizing (a starch added to fabrics during the weaving process), and relaxes the fabric so it hangs with the grain straight. Another approach is to use a product called Retayne, which will fix any excess dye into the fabric.

After washing, I hang the fabric on a drying rack, taking care to fold the fabric in half lengthwise and align the selvages so the fabric dries flat and straight. A clothes dryer is another option.

Once dry, fold the fabrics in half lengthwise, wrong sides together, and line up the selvages, making sure that the two edges align as closely as possible. This will prevent any wrinkling or twisting of the fabric. The aim is to have the grain of the fabric, called the warp, running straight up and down at a right angle to the cross-woven threads, called the weft.

No matter how carefully a fabric is cut at the store, there is likely to be some distortion of the weave due to the way fabrics are manufactured. So keep in mind, the selvages will be straight even if the cut edge is not.

Press the folded fabric on both sides, taking care not to press the fold line, since the crease can be very difficult to remove.

Cutting Strips

The first step in cutting straight strips is to straighten the cut edge of your fabric. After washing, the edge is usually slightly frayed and a bit crooked.

1 Lay the folded fabric on a cutting mat with the fold closest to you. Align the fold with a line on the mat and place the uneven edges to your right. (Reverse these directions if you're left-handed.) Smooth out the fabric to make sure there are no wrinkles. The uneven edge should just cover a line running across the cutting mat.

2 Place a 6" × 24" ruler along the right edge of the fabric, with a horizontal line of the ruler aligned with the fold and the right cutting edge just inside all the layers of fabric. Starting at the fold, make a cut by sliding the cutter away from you along the long edge of the ruler. The fold of the fabric and the newly cut edge should be at a right angle to each other. If you haven't already created your fabric guide, you can make one using the slivers of fabric cut off when straightening the edges.

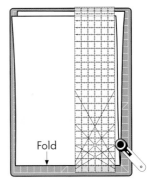

Fold

3 Turn the fabric over so that the fold is still closest to you but the cut edge is to your left. Smooth out the fabric to eliminate any wrinkles. To cut a strip, place the long ruler so it overlaps the fabric, aligning the marking for the desired width even with the cut (left) edge of the fabric. For example, to cut a 2½" strip, place the 2½" line on the ruler along the newly cut edge of the fabric. (Note that the project instructions list the width and number of strips you'll need to cut.) The folded edge of the fabric should align with a horizontal line of the ruler. If it doesn't, repeat step 2. You want your strips to be precisely perpendicular to the fold. If they're not, your cut strips will be V-shaped, not straight.

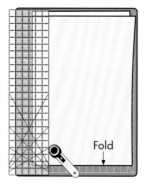

If you're working with fat quarters or fat eighths, use the selvage, instead of the fold, as your reference edge for straightening the fabric. Should the selvage be crooked, you can usually make out the straight grain on the wrong side of the fabric to use as your reference, although this doesn't work so well with batiks.

Mark the Strips

You may find it helpful to lightly write the fabric number on the wrong side of each strip, near the selvage, using a water-soluble marker. This way you can cut your strips and sort them into strip set groups at the same time.

Sewing Strip Sets

After selecting and cutting your fabrics, the next step is to make the strip sets. By this stage you have already decided on the fabric order for the finished project, and you have created a fabric guide showing each individual fabric alongside its fabric number.

Each project in the book tells you how many strips to cut and how to arrange the cut strips into strip sets. For every project except Spinning Wheel Tree Skirt on page 36, the strips will be arranged in numerical order. As you sew, refer to your fabric guide often to make sure you don't get the order mixed up.

1 Select one strip set. To avoid getting the strips out of sequence, stack all the folded strips in numerical order with the selvages toward you.

Stack folded strips.

2 Peel back the top layer of strip 1, then pick up the other end along with the top layer of strip 2. Align the ends of the strips, with strip 2 on top. Begin stitching on a small scrap of fabric and sew to its edge. Then sew the two strips together along their long edges. Don't snip the thread at the end of the seam.

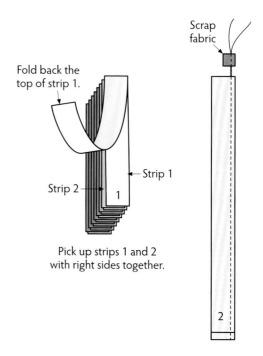

Pick up strips 1 and 2 with right sides together.

Sewing Accurate ¼" Seams

Whatever method you use to indicate where the edge of the fabric should be when you're sewing a ¼" seam allowance, it's best to check that the resulting seam allowances really are only a scant ¼" wide.

To check your seam allowance, cut three 1½" × 6" fabric strips. Sew the three pieces together along their long edges. Press the seam allowances in one direction and measure the center strip, which should be 1" wide.

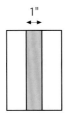

If the center strip isn't exactly 1" along the entire strip, you need to adjust the way you're sewing your seams. If the width of the center strip varies, meaning the seamlines are wavy, you'll find it helpful to practice sewing straight seams. If the width of the center strip is uniformly less than 1", your seam allowance is too wide. If the center strip is uniformly more than 1" wide, your seam allowance is too narrow.

3 Pick up the next two strips the same way as before, aligning the ends. Sew the second pair of strips together with just a short gap, no more than ¼", between the end of one pair of strips and the next. This is called chain piecing and saves a lot of thread. Continue in this manner,

with the even-numbered strip always on top, until all the strips in that group are sewn together in pairs.

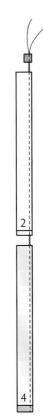

4 When all the strips are in pairs, sew onto a small scrap of fabric. Cut the threads between each of the strip pairs, stacking them on top of the last pair sewn, and keeping the even-numbered strip on top with all the seams pointing away from you.

5 Lay one strip pair on your ironing surface and press the seamline only once to set it.

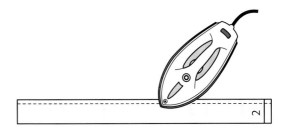

6 Open the strip pair so the fabrics are right side up. Using the tip and edge of your iron, gently push the even-numbered strip away from the odd-numbered strip along the seamline. Pressing the seams this way helps prevent a small pleat from forming next to the seam and distorting your strip set.

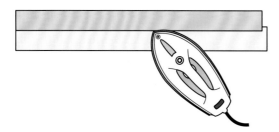

7 All of the remaining seams should be sewn from the uneven end of the paired strips. If you sew all the seams from the aligned, or even, end, you may end up with a bowed strip set. To prevent this, start by arranging the strip pairs in the correct sequence and line up the even ends of the first two strip pairs. Flip the paired strips over and sew them together along their long edges, starting at the *uneven ends*. As you sew, notice that the even-numbered strip is on top again. Chain piece the remaining strip pairs in the same way, and then press the new seam allowances as you did before.

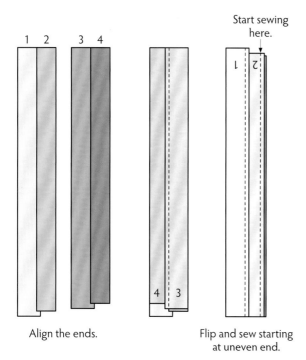

Align the ends.

Start sewing here.

Flip and sew starting at uneven end.

Pressing Seam Allowances

Pressing as described here will result in a strip set with the seam allowances pressed toward the highest-numbered fabric. To make a strip set with the seam allowances pressed toward the lowest number, turn the stack of strip pairs over end to end so the odd-numbered strip is on top before pressing the strips.

Once four or more strips are joined, you can ensure that each new seam allowance will lie in the same direction as the others by checking that the existing seam allowances on the top layer of strips are pointing toward you, and the seam to be pressed is pointing away from you.

8 After sewing the first two strip pairs together, you'll be sewing from the uneven end until all strip pairs are sewn into a single strip set. Don't be concerned if the aligned edge is a little uneven.

There is no rule that says you must make all the strip sets before beginning to make the project. I work more quickly if I make two strip sets at a time—one with seam allowances pressed toward the lowest fabric number and the other with seam allowances pressed toward the highest fabric number—and use them before making two more strip sets. You may discover that you prefer to make all the strip sets before starting to crosscut them into segments.

However, when making bargello blocks, one segment from each different strip set is required for every block, so you need to make at least one of every strip set before you can start making the blocks. Dancing Butterflies on page 63 is made with seven different strip sets. Similarly, circular bargello projects can use as many as 18 different strip sets, depending on the number of colors used and the angle of the wedges. For circular

Why Does Pressing Direction Matter?

If you're new to bargello patchwork, you may wonder why seam allowances should be pressed either up or down and why they should lie in opposite directions in adjacent bargello strips. Bargello quilts have a lot of seams, which add considerable bulk to the finished item. Having the seam allowances pressed up in one segment and down in the adjacent segment allows the seams to nest into one another, helping to lessen the bulk of the surface. Additionally, nested seams are easy to match because you can feel when they are properly interlocked as you sew the seams between the segments.

Nest the seams.

If the seam allowances lie on top of one another, you will have six layers of fabric to stitch through when joining bargello strips and when quilting. Sewing through that many layers is a good way to break a needle, not to mention ending up with a lumpy quilt.

You may think that it would help to press the seam allowances open, but there are three distinct disadvantages to this:

- Seam allowances that are pressed open are not as structurally strong as those pressed in one direction. The seams can separate or tear more easily, leading to a shorter lifespan for the quilt.

- Seam allowances that are pressed open are difficult to match when joining adjacent segments, meaning that the seams may not line up.

- It takes quite a lot of extra time to press the seam allowances open. Pressing them in one direction is much quicker.

projects, one of every different strip set is needed before you can begin sewing the wedges together. The Spinning Wheel Tree Skirt on page 36 uses only six colors and 15° wedges, and requires only six different strip sets.

Cutting Strip Sets

Now that you've sewn your strip sets—or some of them, at least—it's time to start cutting segments to make the bargello columns for your chosen project. Refer to the project instructions and design table to determine whether the seam allowances should be pressed toward the lowest fabric number or highest fabric number, and then select the appropriate strip set.

1 Fold the strip set in half, right sides together. Lightly press the seam where the strip set is folded. This helps to ensure the strip set will lie flat on your cutting mat and the seams will nest together.

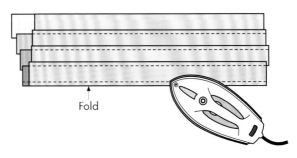

Fold

2 Before cutting segments, straighten the edge of the strip set by placing the folded strip set on your cutting mat with the folded edge closest to you and the aligned edge to your right. Line up the edge of the pressed seam allowance on one of the lines on the mat, smoothing out the strip set. Make sure there are no wrinkles and the strips are lying parallel to each other and to the lines on the mat. Place your ruler on the strip set, with a horizontal line of the ruler aligned with a seamline and the right cutting edge inside the layers of the strip set. Cut along the long right edge of the ruler.

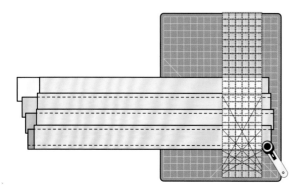

3 Turn the strip set over so the fold is still closest to you and the straightened edge is on the left. Smooth out the strip set once more to eliminate any wrinkles. Cut the number of segments required in the width indicated in the design table.

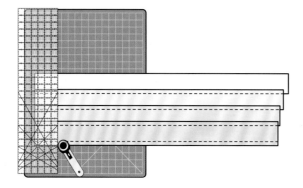

4 To cut the segments for the next column, repeat steps 1–3 using a strip set with the seam allowances pressed in the opposite direction.

If bargello techniques are new to you, consider choosing Dreamland's Curtain on page 15 as your introduction. It's the most beginner-friendly project in the book because the strip sets are sewn into loops and you cut only one segment for each column.

Keep Track with Paper Labels

Before beginning a project, refer to the project's design table and make a label for each column by writing the column number on a small piece of paper. Pin the appropriate label on each column as you complete it.

When it comes time to swap one strip set for another on your cutting table, paper labels will again come in handy. Instead of constantly swapping one strip set for another on your cutting mat, cut as many segments as you can from one strip set with the seams pressed in one direction. Then cut segments from a strip set with the seam allowances pressed in the opposite direction. To keep track of the segments, write the corresponding column number on a small piece of paper and pin it to the stack of segments.

Dreamland's Curtain

Inspired by quilts I made for my twin granddaughters when they turned two, this version brought back memories of the joy on the girls' faces when I gave them their "Granny quilts." Using a pack of gorgeous pastels and supplementing with a few more fabrics, I was able to achieve the size I wanted, making this perfect for a baby quilt.

Fabric Selection

This sweet little quilt uses 24 different pastel fabrics that blend from one color to the next.

Materials

Yardage is based on 42"-wide fabric. Fat eighths measure 9" × 21".

24 fat eighths of assorted pastel prints for bargello (fabrics 1–24)

⅜ yard of gray tone on tone for binding

1¼ yards of fabric for backing

40" × 41" piece of batting

Cutting

All measurements include ¼"-wide seam allowances.

From *each* of fabrics 1–24, cut:
3 strips, 2" × 21"

From *each* of fabrics 12 and 24, cut:
1 strip, 2" × 21"; crosscut into 1 square, 2" × 2"

From *each* of fabrics 14 and 22, cut:
1 strip, 2" × 21"; crosscut into 2 squares, 2" × 2"

From the gray tone on tone, cut:
4 strips, 2¼" × 42"

Preparation

Referring to "Preparing a Fabric Guide" on page 8, assemble a fabric guide using a scrap of each of the 24 fabrics. Arrange them in order from 1 to 24. This will ensure the fabrics are in the right order when making the strip sets.

Prepare a set of labels for columns 1–28 (*column 1, column 2,* etc.) to pin on the completed columns.

Making the Strip Sets

1 Referring to "Sewing Strip Sets" on page 10 and using the 2"-wide strips, sort the strips into three groups, with one strip of each fabric in each group. Arrange the strips in each group in numerical order. Sew the strips in each group together to make three strip sets. Press the seam

allowances toward fabric 1 on two strip sets and toward fabric 24 on the remaining strip set.

Fabric 1		Fabric 1
Fabric 2		Fabric 2
Fabric 3		Fabric 3
Fabric 4		Fabric 4
Fabric 5		Fabric 5
Fabric 6		Fabric 6
Fabric 7		Fabric 7
Fabric 8		Fabric 8
Fabric 9		Fabric 9
Fabric 10		Fabric 10
Fabric 11		Fabric 11
Fabric 12		Fabric 12
Fabric 13		Fabric 13
Fabric 14		Fabric 14
Fabric 15		Fabric 15
Fabric 16		Fabric 16
Fabric 17		Fabric 17
Fabric 18		Fabric 18
Fabric 19		Fabric 19
Fabric 20		Fabric 20
Fabric 21		Fabric 21
Fabric 22		Fabric 22
Fabric 23		Fabric 23
Fabric 24		Fabric 24

Make 2.   Make 1.

2 Fold each strip set in half lengthwise, right sides together, carefully matching the long edges of fabrics 1 and 24 to make a tube. Make sure the tube lies flat and straight and isn't skewed. Sew along the raw edges using a ¼" seam allowance. Carefully press the seam allowances in the same direction as the others in the strip set.

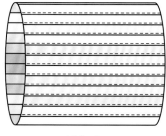

Make 3.

Cutting Segments

When cutting the strip sets into segments, be sure to nest the seam allowances between the strips. If the seam allowances are lying on top of one another, you won't be able to cut the segments evenly.

Making Column 1

Refer to "Cutting Strip Sets" on page 13 for more information as needed.

1 Cut one 2½"-wide segment from a strip set with the seam allowances pressed toward fabric 1.

2 Turn loop right side out. Use a seam ripper to remove the stitching between fabrics 1 and 24.

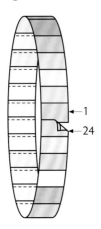

3 Pin the column 1 label to the top of the completed column.

Making Column 2

1 Cut one 2"-wide segment from a strip set with the seam allowances pressed toward fabric 1.

2 Turn the loop right side out. Use a seam ripper to remove the stitching between fabrics 23 and 24.

3 Sew the 2" square of fabric 24 to fabric 23 at the bottom of the column. Press the seam allowances toward fabric 1.

4 Pin the column 2 label to the top of the completed column.

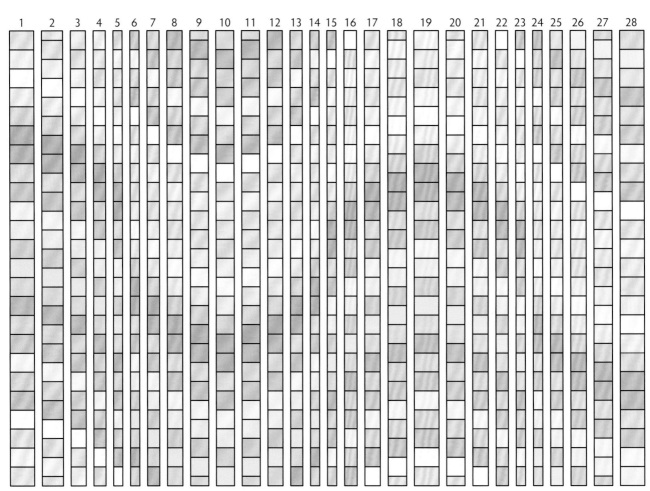

Quilt layout

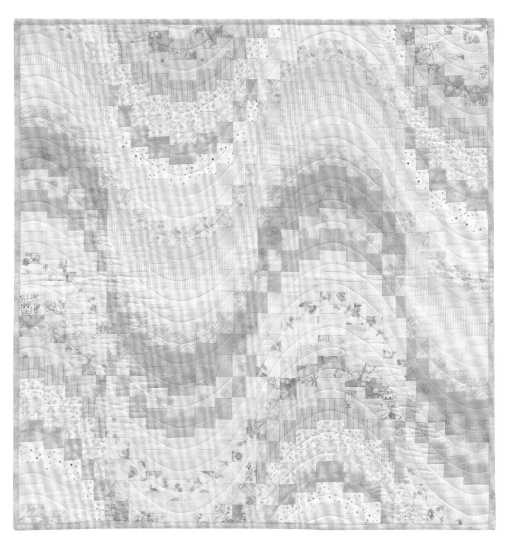

FINISHED SIZE: 35½" × 36½"

Pieced and quilted by Judith Steele.

Stepping Up or Down

Some of the columns in this quilt are stepped up or down half of the strip width rather than a full strip width. Therefore, there isn't a seam-allowance intersection to use as a matching point when joining the columns. The seamline of a subsequent column falls at the midpoint of each strip in the previous column. For columns 2, 9, 11, 18, 20, and 27, half of the patch at both the top and bottom of the column will extend beyond the adjacent column.

Working from the Design Table

Continue working in the same manner, cutting one segment for each column in the width indicated in the Dreamland's Curtain design tables on pages 20 and 21. Referring to your fabric guide and using the bold lines on the design table as a reference, remove the stitching between the fabrics, as needed, making sure to select the strip set with the seam allowances pressed in the direction indicated on the table. For columns 9, 11, 18, 20, and 27, add the 2" square of each fabric indicated in the design table, pressing the seam allowances in the same direction as the other seam allowances. For all columns, pin the appropriate label to the top of the column.

Assembling the Quilt Top

1 Place columns 1 and 2 right sides together, with the seamlines of column 2 halfway between the seamlines of column 1. Join the columns along the long edge. Press the seam allowances toward column 1.

2 Sew column 3 to column 2, right sides together, with the seamlines on column 3 halfway between the seamlines on column 2. Press the seam allowances toward column 2.

3 Add columns 4–8 in numerical order, carefully matching the seam intersections. Press the seam allowances toward the lowest numbered column.

4 Referring to the design table, sew the remaining columns together in pairs, making sure to either stagger the seamlines or match the seam intersections as indicated on the design table. Press the seam allowances toward the lowest-numbered column.

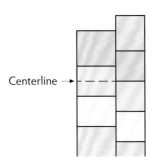

Centerline →

Design Table: Dreamland's Curtain

Column	1	2	3	4	5	6	7	8	9	10	11	12	13	14
Cut width of segments	2½"	2"	1¾"	1½"	1¼"	1¼"	1½"	1¾"	2"	2½"	2"	1¾"	1½"	1¼"
Pressing direction	↑	↑	↑	↓	↑	↓	↑	↓	↑	↑	↑	↑	↓	↑
Fabric number	1	24	24	23	22	17	16	15	14	14	14	15	16	17
	2	1	1	24	23	18	17	16	15	15	15	16	17	18
	3	2	2	1	24	19	18	17	16	16	16	17	18	19
	4	3	3	2	1	20	19	18	17	17	17	18	19	20
	5	4	4	3	2	21	20	19	18	18	18	19	20	21
	6	5	5	4	3	22	21	20	19	19	19	20	21	22
	7	6	6	5	4	23	22	21	20	20	20	21	22	23
	8	7	7	6	5	24	23	22	21	21	21	22	23	24
	9	8	8	7	6	1	24	23	22	22	22	23	24	1
	10	9	9	8	7	2	1	24	23	23	23	24	1	2
	11	10	10	9	8	3	2	1	24	24	24	1	2	3
	12	11	11	10	9	4	3	2	1	1	1	2	3	4
	13	12	12	11	10	5	4	3	2	2	2	3	4	5
	14	13	13	12	11	6	5	4	3	3	3	4	5	6
	15	14	14	13	12	7	6	5	4	4	4	5	6	7
	16	15	15	14	13	8	7	6	5	5	5	6	7	8
	17	16	16	15	14	9	8	7	6	6	6	7	8	9
	18	17	17	16	15	10	9	8	7	7	7	8	9	10
	19	18	18	17	16	11	10	9	8	8	8	9	10	11
	20	19	19	18	17	12	11	10	9	9	9	10	11	12
	21	20	20	19	18	13	12	11	10	10	10	11	12	13
	22	21	21	20	19	14	13	12	11	11	11	12	13	14
	23	22	22	21	20	15	14	13	12	12	12	13	14	15
	24	23	23	22	21	16	15	14	13	13	13	14	15	16

5 Sew the column pairs together, flipping them over and sewing from the opposite ends of the columns. Continue joining the pairs, paying careful attention to the design table for seam placement, until all the columns have been sewn together.

6 Straighten the top and bottom edges, trimming off the pieces that extend beyond the edges of the other columns.

Finishing the Quilt

For more details on any finishing steps, go to ShopMartingale.com/HowtoQuilt to download free illustrated information.

1 Layer the quilt top with batting and backing; baste. Machine quilt a decorative design across the surface of the quilt (or take the top and backing to a professional long-arm machine quilter).

2 Add a label.

3 Using the gray 2¼"-wide strips, make the binding and attach it to the quilt.

Column	15	16	17	18	19	20	21	22	23	24	25	26	27	28
Cut width of segments	1¼"	1½"	1¾"	2"	2½"	2"	1¾"	1½"	1¼"	1¼"	1½"	1¾"	2"	2½"
Pressing direction	↓	↑	↓	↑	↓	↑	↑	↓	↑	↓	↑	↓	↑	↑
Fabric number	20	21	22	22	23	22	22	21	20	15	14	13	12	12
	21	22	23	23	24	23	23	22	21	16	15	14	13	13
	22	23	24	24	1	24	24	23	22	17	16	15	14	14
	23	24	1	1	2	1	1	24	23	18	17	16	15	15
	24	1	2	2	3	2	2	1	24	19	18	17	16	16
	1	2	3	3	4	3	3	2	1	20	19	18	17	17
	2	3	4	4	5	4	4	3	2	21	20	19	18	18
	3	4	5	5	6	5	5	4	3	22	21	20	19	19
	4	5	6	6	7	6	6	5	4	23	22	21	20	20
	5	6	7	7	8	7	7	6	5	24	23	22	21	21
	6	7	8	8	9	8	8	7	6	1	24	23	22	22
	7	8	9	9	10	9	9	8	7	2	1	24	23	23
	8	9	10	10	11	10	10	9	8	3	2	1	24	24
	9	10	11	11	12	11	11	10	9	4	3	2	1	1
	10	11	12	12	13	12	12	11	10	5	4	3	2	2
	11	12	13	13	14	13	13	12	11	6	5	4	3	3
	12	13	14	14	15	14	14	13	12	7	6	5	4	4
	13	14	15	15	16	15	15	14	13	8	7	6	5	5
	14	15	16	16	17	16	16	15	14	9	8	7	6	6
	15	16	17	17	18	17	17	16	15	10	9	8	7	7
	16	17	18	18	19	18	18	17	16	11	10	9	8	8
	17	18	19	19	20	19	19	18	17	12	11	10	9	9
	18	19	20	20	21	20	20	19	18	13	12	11	10	10
	19	20	21	21	22	21	21	20	19	14	13	12	11	11

Autumn Leaves

Requiring only 10 different fabrics, this table runner is a perfect project for learning the bargello technique. I originally made it in shades of blues and teals as a birthday gift for my younger daughter, but I like the bold contrast of blacks and yellows much better.

Fabric Selection

This table runner uses 10 fabrics in two color groups. The first group consists of six fabrics, including batiks and a subtle stripe, ranging from orange to pale yellow. The second group consists of four black-and-white (or black-and-cream) small-scale prints, ranging from dark to light.

Materials

Yardage is based on 42"-wide fabric. Fat quarters measure 18" × 21".

6 fat quarters of assorted yellow and orange batiks, stripes, or prints for bargello and outer border (fabrics 1–6)

4 fat quarters of assorted black-and-white or black-and-cream prints for bargello and outer border (fabrics 7–10)

1 fat quarter of orange batik for inner border

⅜ yard of orange print for binding

1¼ yards of fabric for backing

21" × 53" piece of batting

Cutting

All measurements include ¼"-wide seam allowances.

From *each* of fabrics 1–10, cut:
5 strips, 2" × 21"

From the orange batik for inner border, cut:
7 strips, 1¼" × 21"

From the orange print for binding, cut:
4 strips, 2¼" × 42"

FINISHED SIZE: 17" × 48½"
Pieced and quilted by Judith Steele.

Preparation

Referring to "Preparing a Fabric Guide" on page 8, assemble a fabric guide using a scrap of each of the 10 fabrics. Arrange them in order from the most intense orange (fabric 1) to the palest yellow (fabric 6) to the darkest black with white or cream (fabric 10). This will ensure the fabrics are in the right order when making the strip sets.

Prepare a set of labels for columns 1–11 (*column 1, column 2,* etc.) to pin on the completed columns.

Making the Strip Sets

Referring to "Sewing Strip Sets" on page 10 and using the 2"-wide strips, sort the strips into five groups, with one strip of each fabric in each group. Arrange the strips in each group in numerical order. Sew the strips in each group together to make five strip sets that measure 15½" × 21". Press the seam allowances toward fabric 1 on two strip sets and toward fabric 10 on the remaining three strip sets.

| Fabric 1 |
| Fabric 2 |
| Fabric 3 |
| Fabric 4 |
| Fabric 5 |
| Fabric 6 |
| Fabric 7 |
| Fabric 8 |
| Fabric 9 |
| Fabric 10 |

Make 2.

| Fabric 1 |
| Fabric 2 |
| Fabric 3 |
| Fabric 4 |
| Fabric 5 |
| Fabric 6 |
| Fabric 7 |
| Fabric 8 |
| Fabric 9 |
| Fabric 10 |

Make 3.

Making Columns 1 and 11

Refer to "Cutting Strip Sets" on page 13 for more information as needed.

1 Cut three ⅞"-wide segments from a strip set with the seam allowances pressed toward fabric 10.

2 Sew fabric 10 on the first segment to fabric 1 on the second segment.

3 Sew fabric 1 on the third segment to fabric 10 on the second segment. Compare your finished column to column 1 of the Autumn Leaves design table on page 29. The numbers assigned to your fabrics should match the numbers in the table, and you should have 30 fabrics in your column. Pin the column 1 label to the top of the finished column. Press all seam allowances toward the bottom of the column.

4 Repeat steps 1–3 to make an identical column, and label it *column 11*.

Making Column 2

1 Cut four 1¼"-wide segments from a strip set with the seam allowances pressed toward fabric 1.

2 Sew fabric 10 on the first segment to fabric 1 on the second segment. Then sew the ends (fabrics 1 and 10) together to make a loop.

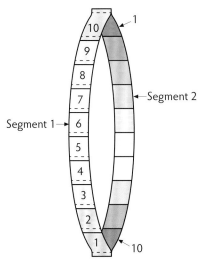

Join to make a loop.

3 Turn the loop right side out. Use a seam ripper to remove the stitching between fabrics 8 and 9 and between fabrics 9 and 10 on the second segment. Reserve the fabric 9 piece to use later. Fabric 8 will be at the bottom of the column.

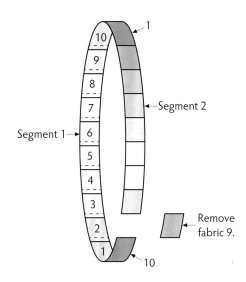

Remove fabric 9.

4 Sew fabric 1 on the third segment to fabric 8 on the second segment.

5 Sew fabric 1 on the fourth segment to fabric 10 on the third segment.

6 Remove the stitching between fabrics 1 and 2 on the fourth segment. Reserve the 2–10 piece for the second half of the table runner and the outer border.

7 Press all seam allowances toward the top of the column. Compare your finished column to column 2 of the design table. The numbers assigned to your fabrics should match the numbers in the table, and you should have 30 fabrics in your column. Pin the column 2 label to the top of the column.

Making Column 3

1 Cut four 1⅝"-wide segments from a strip set with the seam allowances pressed toward fabric 10.

2 Sew fabric 10 on the first segment to fabric 1 on the second segment. Sew the ends (fabrics 1 and 10) together to make a loop.

3 Turn the fabric loop right side out. Remove the stitching between fabrics 6 and 7 and between fabrics 8 and 9 on the second segment. Reserve the two-fabric piece to use later. Fabric 6 will be at the bottom of the column.

4 Sew fabric 1 on the third segment to fabric 6 on the second segment. Fabric 10 will now be at the bottom of the column.

5 Sew fabric 10 on the third segment to fabric 1 on the fourth segment.

6 Remove the stitching between fabrics 2 and 3 on the fourth segment. Reserve the 3–10 piece for the second half of the table runner and the outer border.

7 Press all seam allowances toward the bottom of the column. Compare your finished column to column 3 of the design table. The numbers assigned to your fabrics should match the numbers in the table, and you should have 30 fabrics in your column. Pin the column 3 label to the top of the column.

Working from the Design Table

1 Continue working in the same manner, cutting four segments each for columns 4, 5, and 7–10 in the widths indicated in the design table. Cut three 2¾"-wide segments for column 6. When constructing columns 7–10, you may be able to use some of the reserved pieces from previous columns, if they're the correct width. Referring to your fabric guide and using the bold lines on the design table as a reference, remove the stitching between fabrics, as needed, and join the segments in the order indicated for the column you are making.

2 After completing each new column, compare it to the design table to make sure the fabric numbers and pressing direction are accurate. Then pin the appropriate label to the top of the column.

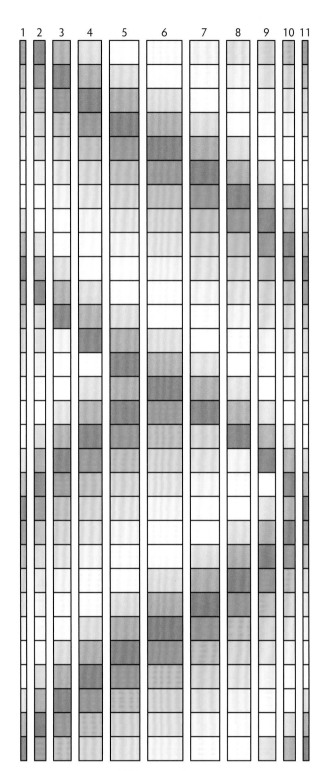

Table-runner layout

Joining the Columns

1 With right sides together and starting with columns 1 and 2, join the columns in pairs, sewing along their long edges and carefully matching the seam intersections. Press the seam allowances toward the odd-numbered columns.

2 Join the pairs and press the seam allowances toward the lower-numbered columns. Continue in this manner until all the columns have been joined.

Adding the Inner Border

1 Join the orange batik 1¼"-wide strips end to end and press the seam allowances open. Measure the length of the table runner through the center. From the pieced strip, cut two strips to that length. Sew the strips to the long sides of the table-runner top. Press the seam allowances toward the border strips.

2 Measure across the width of the table runner through the center, including the side borders. From the pieced strip, cut two strips to that measurement and sew them to the ends of the table runner. Press the seam allowances toward the border strips. The table-runner top should measure 15½" × 47", including the seam allowances.

Adding the Outer Border

Refer to the border diagrams at right.

1 From the remaining strip sets, cut nine 1¼"-wide segments.

2 For the left outer border, you will use four segments. On the first segment, remove the stitching between fabrics 1 and 2 and between fabrics 3 and 4. Sew fabric 3 on the two-piece segment to fabric 10 on the second segment. Fabric 2 will be at the bottom of the strip. Sew fabric 1 on the third segment to fabric 2 at the bottom of the strip. Sew fabric 1 on the fourth

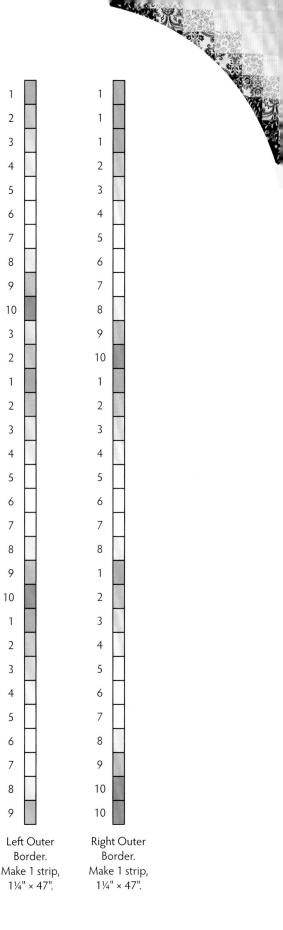

Left Outer
Border.
Make 1 strip,
1¼" × 47".

Right Outer
Border.
Make 1 strip,
1¼" × 47".

segment to fabric 10 at the bottom of the strip. Remove the stitching between fabrics 9 and 10 at the bottom of the strip. Discard the fabric 10 piece. Trim the border strip to 1¼" × 47", including seam allowances.

3 For the right outer border, you will use the remaining five segments. Sew fabric 10 on the first segment to fabric 1 on the second segment. Remove the stitching between fabrics 8 and 9. Fabric 8 will be at the bottom of the strip. Sew fabric 8 on the second segment to fabric 1 on the third segment. On the fourth and fifth segments, remove the stitching between fabrics 1 and 2 and between fabrics 9 and 10. Sew both fabric 1 pieces to fabric 1 at the top of the strip. Sew one fabric 10 piece to fabric 10 at the bottom of the strip. Trim the border strip to measure 1¼" × 47", including seam allowances.

4 Making sure the color placement is correct, sew the left and right borders to the sides of the table-runner top. Press the seam allowances toward the inner border. The table-runner top should measure 17" × 47", including seam allowances.

5 For the top border, use the reserved pieces in the sizes and fabric numbers listed. (If you don't have enough reserved pieces, you can cut pieces from the scraps of the fat quarters.) Then join the pieces in the following order to make a 1¼" × 17" border strip.

Fabric 1: 1¼" × 2" rectangle

Fabric 10: 1¼" × ⅞" rectangle

Fabric 9: 1¼" × 1¼" square

Fabric 8: 1¼" × 1⅝" rectangle

Fabric 7: 1¼" × 2" rectangle

Fabric 6: 1¼" × 2⅜" rectangle

Fabric 5: 1¼" × 2¾" rectangle

Fabric 4: 1¼" × 2⅜" rectangle

Fabric 3: 1¼" × 2" rectangle

Fabric 2: 1¼" × 1⅝" rectangle

Fabric 1: 1¼" × 2⅜" rectangle

Fabric 10: 1¼" × 1¼" square

Top Outer Border.
Make 1 strip,
1¼" × 17".

6 For the bottom border, use the reserved pieces in the sizes and fabric numbers listed. (If you don't have enough reserved pieces, you can cut pieces from the scraps of the fat quarters.) Then join the pieces in the following order to make a 1¼" × 17" border strip.

Fabric 10: 1¼" × 1¼" square

Fabric 1: 1¼" × 1¼" square

Fabric 2: 1¼" × 1⅝" rectangle

Fabric 3: 1¼" × 1⅝" rectangle

Fabric 4: 1¼" × 2" rectangle

Fabric 5: 1¼" × 2⅜" rectangle

Fabric 6: 1¼" × 2¾" rectangle

Fabric 7: 1¼" × 2⅜" rectangle

Fabric 8: 1¼" × 2" rectangle

Fabric 9: 1¼" × 1⅝" rectangle

Fabric 10: 1¼" × 3⅛" rectangle

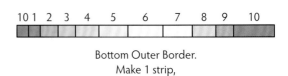

Bottom Outer Border.
Make 1 strip,
1¼" × 17".

7 Referring to the photo on page 23 and making sure the color placement is correct, sew the top and bottom borders to the table-runner top. Press the seam allowances toward the inner border. The table runner should measure 17" × 48½".

Finishing the Table Runner

For more details on any finishing steps, go to ShopMartingale.com/HowtoQuilt to download free illustrated information.

1 Layer the table-runner top with backing and batting; baste. Machine quilt in the ditch (or take the top and backing to a professional long-arm machine quilter).

2 Add a label.

3 Using the orange print 2¼"-wide strips, make the binding and attach it to the table runner.

Design Table: Autumn Leaves

Column	1	2	3	4	5	6	7	8	9	10	11
Cut width of segments	⅞"	1¼"	1⅝"	2"	2⅜"	2¾"	2⅜"	2"	1⅝"	1¼"	⅞"
Pressing direction	↓	↑	↓	↑	↓	↑	↓	↑	↓	↑	↓
Number of segments to cut	3	4	4	4	4	3	4	4	4	4	3
Fabric number	1	10	9	8	7	6	5	4	3	2	1
	2	1	10	9	8	7	6	5	4	3	2
	3	2	1	10	9	8	7	6	5	4	3
	4	3	2	1	10	9	8	7	6	5	4
	5	4	3	2	1	10	9	8	7	6	5
	6	5	4	3	2	1	10	9	8	7	6
	7	6	5	4	3	2	1	10	9	8	7
	8	7	6	5	4	3	2	1	10	9	8
	9	8	7	6	5	4	3	2	1	10	9
	10	9	8	7	6	5	4	3	2	1	10
	1	10	9	8	7	6	5	4	3	2	1
	2	1	10	9	8	7	6	5	4	1	2
	3	2	1	10	9	8	7	6	1	2	3
	4	3	2	1	10	9	8	1	2	3	4
	5	4	3	2	1	10	1	2	3	4	5
	6	5	4	3	2	1	2	3	4	5	6
	7	6	5	4	1	2	3	4	5	6	7
	8	7	6	1	2	3	4	5	6	7	8
	9	8	1	2	3	4	5	6	7	8	9
	10	1	2	3	4	5	6	7	8	9	10
	1	2	3	4	5	6	7	8	9	10	1
	2	3	4	5	6	7	8	9	10	1	2
	3	4	5	6	7	8	9	10	1	2	3
	4	5	6	7	8	9	10	1	2	3	4
	5	6	7	8	9	10	1	2	3	4	5
	6	7	8	9	10	1	2	3	4	5	6
	7	8	9	10	1	2	3	4	5	6	7
	8	9	10	1	2	3	4	5	6	7	8
	9	10	1	2	3	4	5	6	7	8	9
	10	1	2	3	4	5	6	7	8	9	10

Diamond Star Tote

I designed this shoulder bag for a sewing class I was teaching. It's a quick project to make and can be completed in a weekend. For quite some time now I've been carrying the prototype I made for the class, and I find it to be one of the most useful totes I've ever had.

Fabric Selection

You'll only need four fabrics for this tote. To make the diamond pattern really shine, aim for high contrast between the lightest and darkest green prints.

Materials

Yardage is based on 42"-wide fabric. Fat quarters measure 18" × 21".

4 fat quarters of assorted green prints for bargello and handles (fabrics 1–4)
⅝ yard of complementary fabric for lining and handles
20" × 31" rectangle of batting

Cutting

All measurements include ¼"-wide seam allowances.

From *each* of fabrics 1–4, cut:
7 strips, 2" × 21"

From the lining fabric, cut:
2 strips, 2¼" × 30½"
1 rectangle, 15" × 27½"

From the batting, cut:
2 strips, 1½" × 30½"
1 rectangle, 16" × 29"

Preparation

Referring to "Preparing a Fabric Guide" on page 8, assemble a fabric guide using a scrap of each of the four fabrics. Arrange them in order from the lightest (fabric 1) to the darkest green (fabric 4). This will ensure the fabrics are in the right order when making the strip sets.

Prepare a set of labels for columns 1–9 (*column 1, column 2,* etc.) to pin on the completed columns.

Making the Strip Sets

1 Referring to "Sewing Strip Sets" on page 10 and using the 2"-wide strips, sort the strips into seven groups, with one strip of each fabric in each group. Arrange the strips in each group in numerical order.

Sew the strips in each group together to make seven strip sets that measure 6½" × 21". Press the seam allowances toward fabric 4.

| Fabric 1 |
| Fabric 2 |
| Fabric 3 |
| Fabric 4 |

Make 7.

2 Referring to "Cutting Strip Sets" on page 13, cut the following segments to make the columns for the front of the tote:

Columns 1 and 9: 6 segments, 3" × 6½"

Columns 2 and 8: 4 segments, 2½" × 6½"

Columns 3 and 7: 4 segments, 2" × 6½"

Columns 4 and 6: 4 segments, 1½" × 6½"

Column 5: 3 segments, 1" × 6½"

3 Repeat step 2 to cut the segments for the back of the tote.

Making Columns 1 and 9

Refer to your fabric guide and use the bold lines on the Diamond Star Tote design table on page 35 as a reference.

1 Using two 3"-wide segments, sew fabric 1 on the first segment to fabric 4 on the second segment. On the second segment, remove the stitching between fabrics 3 and 4. Set aside the leftover segment for column 2.

2 Sew fabric 1 on the third segment to fabric 4 on the second segment. Press all the seam allowances in the same direction. Pin the column 1 label to the top of the finished column.

3 Repeat steps 1 and 2 to make an identical column, and label it *column 9*.

Making Columns 2 and 8

1 Using the 3"-wide segment left over from making column 1, trim the segment to measure 2½" wide. Remove the stitching between fabrics 2 and 3. Set aside the two-piece segment for column 3.

FINISHED SIZE: 14¼" × 13⅜", excluding handles
Pieced and quilted by Judith Steele.

2 On one of the 2½"-wide segments, sew fabric 1 to fabric 4 to make a small loop. Use another segment to make a second small loop. Turn the loops right side out. Remove the stitching between fabrics 3 and 4 on both loops.

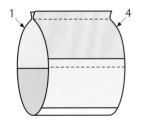
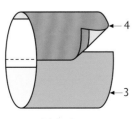

Make 2.

3 Sew the fabric 3 piece from step 1 to fabric 4 on one segment from step 2. Then sew fabric 3 to fabric 4 on the other segment. Compare your column to column 2 of the design table to make sure the fabric numbers match. Press all the seam allowances in the same direction. Pin the column 2 label to the top of the finished column.

4 Repeat steps 1–3 to make an identical column, and label it *column 8*.

Making Columns 3 and 7

1 Using the 2½"-wide segment left over from making column 2, trim the segment to measure 2" wide. Remove the stitching between fabrics 1 and 2. Set aside the fabric 1 piece for column 4.

2 On one of the 2"-wide segments, sew fabric 1 to fabric 4 to make a small loop. Use another segment to make a second small loop. Turn both loops right side out. Remove the stitching between fabrics 2 and 3 on both loops.

3 Sew the fabric 2 piece from step 1 to fabric 3 on one segment from step 2. Then sew fabric 2 to fabric 3 on the other segment. Compare your column to column 3 of the design table to make sure the fabric numbers match. Press all the seam allowances in the same direction. Pin the column 3 label to the top of the finished column.

4 Repeat steps 1–3 to make an identical column, and label it *column 7*.

Making Columns 4 and 6

1 Using the 2"-wide fabric 1 piece left over from making column 3, trim the segment to measure 1½" wide. Save the fabric 1 piece to use in step 4.

2 On one of the 1½"-wide segments, sew fabric 1 to fabric 4 to make a small loop. Turn the loop right side out. Remove the stitching between fabrics 1 and 2.

3 Sew fabric 2 on the first segment to fabric 1 on a second segment.

4 Sew the fabric 1 piece from step 1 to fabric 4 on the second segment. Compare your column to column 4 of the design table to make sure the fabric numbers match. Press all the seam allowances in the same direction. Pin the column 4 label to the top of the finished column.

5 Repeat steps 1–4 to make an identical column, and label it *column 6*.

Making Column 5

1 Using one of the three 1"-wide segments, remove the stitching between fabrics 3 and 4 on the first segment. Discard the three-piece section.

2 Sew fabric 1 on the second and third segments to the top and bottom of the fabric 4 piece. Compare your column to column 5 of the design table to make sure the fabric numbers match. Pin the column 5 label to the top of the finished column.

Making the Tote Front and Back

1 Referring to the tote layout below, lay out the columns on a flat surface, wrong side up, with all the seam allowances pointing in the same direction. Rotate every other column so the seam allowances point in the opposite direction.

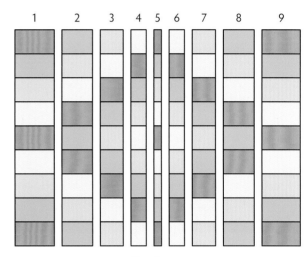

Tote layout

2 Sew the columns together in pairs, and then sew the pairs together. Continue in the same way until all the columns are joined. The completed tote front should measure 14" × 15", including seam allowances. Press the seam allowances in one direction.

3 For the tote back, make columns 1–9 as described in the preceding sections. Then repeat steps 1 and 2 to sew the columns together.

Quilting the Tote

1 Trim the top and bottom of the tote front and back to straighten the edges, if necessary. Sew the front and back together along the bottom edges, right sides together. Press the seam allowances open.

2 Smooth out the 16" × 29" rectangle of batting on a hard, flat surface. Place the tote right side up on top of the batting. Baste the two layers together.

3 Mark the quilting lines on the tote front and back as shown in the quilting plan (or mark a decorative pattern of your choice). Quilt along the marked lines using complementary quilting thread.

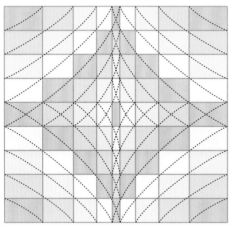

Quilting plan

4 Trim the excess batting even with the edges of the tote.

Assembling the Tote

1 Sew together the tote front and back along both side edges, right sides together and using a ⅜" seam allowance. Trim the bottom corners at an angle and press the seam allowances open.

2 Turn the tote right side out. Fold the top edge under ⅜" and press.

3 Fold the 15" × 27½" lining rectangle in half crosswise, right sides together, and sew along each side using a ⅜" seam allowance. Press the seam allowances open.

4 Place the lining inside the tote, wrong sides together. Fold the top of the lining down between the lining and the tote, adjusting the lining to fit neatly inside the exterior of the tote. Pin the folded edges of the tote and lining together.

Add a Label

If you want to add a label to your tote, write your name and the date on a coordinating scrap of fabric. On the right side of the lining rectangle, place the label at least 1" in from one side and 5" down from one end. Fold the edges under at least ¼" and then edgestitch using matching thread.

Making the Handles

1 From the remaining strip sets, cut 10 segments, 2¼" × 6½".

2 Sew five segments together end to end, joining fabric 1 to fabric 4 to make a handle strip. Press all the seam allowances in one direction. The strip should measure 2¼" × 30½". Make two.

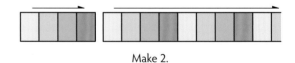

Make 2.

3 Join one lining strip and one handle strip along one long edge. Fold the handle and lining in half, along the seamline, and press flat.

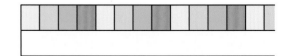

4 Open the strips and place one batting strip on the wrong side of the lining, aligning the edge of the batting with the raw edges of the seam allowances.

5 Turn ¼" of the long, raw edge of the lining over the edge of the batting and press in place.

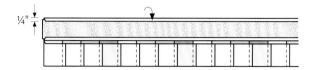

6 Fold the batting and lining over the handle strip and press the seamline. Turn under the long, raw edge of the handle; press and pin in place. The folded edge of the handle and lining should be aligned.

7 Edgestitch along both folded edges. Stitch another three lines along the length of the handle, spacing the lines about ⅜" apart.

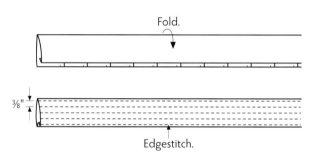

Fold.

Edgestitch.

8 Repeat steps 3–7 to make a second handle.

9 Trim the ends of each handle, making sure the handles are the same length.

Finishing the Tote

1 On both handles, mark 1½" from each end.

2 Mark 2½" in from each side of the tote along the top edge. Mark both front and back.

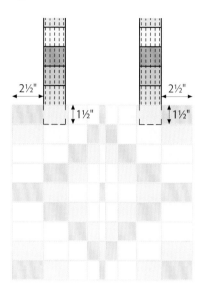

3 Insert the ends of each handle between the lining and the tote, aligning the 1½" mark with the top edge. Pin in place.

4 Sew around the top of the tote, as close to the edge as possible and sewing through all layers. Sew around the top edge two more times, spacing the stitched lines ¼" apart to secure the handles.

Design Table: Diamond Star Tote

Column	1	2	3	4	5	6	7	8	9
Cut width of segments	3"	2½"	2"	1½"	1"	1½"	2"	2½"	3"
Fabric number	4	3	2	1	4	1	2	3	4
	3	2	1	4	3	4	1	2	3
	2	1	4	3	2	3	4	1	2
	1	4	3	2	1	2	3	4	1
	4	3	2	1	4	1	2	3	4
	1	4	3	2	1	2	3	4	1
	2	1	4	3	2	3	4	1	2
	3	2	1	4	3	4	1	2	3
	4	3	2	1	4	1	2	3	4

Spinning Wheel Tree Skirt

Sometimes when we say, "I wonder what would happen if . . . ," something remarkable takes place. I was searching for a way to give a different twist to the usual spiral bargello look, when I wondered what would happen if I reversed the direction of the spiral halfway across the circle. I was amazed at the result, which was intensified by increasing the contrast between the lightest and darkest colors. With only six colors, the pattern repeats four times around the circle, giving the effect of a fast-spinning wheel.

Fabric Selection

You will need six fabrics that represent a vibrant range from light to dark blue.

Materials

Yardage is based on 42"-wide fabric.
1 yard *each* of 6 assorted blue prints for bargello (fabrics 1–6)
¾ yard of blue print for binding
3½ yards of fabric for backing
62" × 62" square of batting
9" × 25" piece of cardboard or template plastic

Cutting

All measurements include ¼"-wide seam allowances.

From *each* of fabrics 1–6, cut:
12 strips, 2½" × 42"

From the blue print for binding, cut:
2¼"-wide bias strips to total 260"

Preparation

Referring to "Preparing a Fabric Guide" on page 8, assemble a fabric guide using a scrap of each of the six fabrics. Arrange them in order from the lightest (fabric 1) to the darkest blue (fabric 6).

Prepare a set of labels for wedge sets 1–12 (*wedge set 1, wedge set 2,* etc.) to pin on the sets of cut wedges.

Trace the wedge pattern sections on pages 43–45 onto cardboard or template plastic. Join the segments to make a complete template and cut it out directly on the line.

Making the Strip Sets

Referring to "Sewing Strip Sets" on page 10 and using the 2½"-wide strips, sort the strips into six groups, with two strips of each fabric in

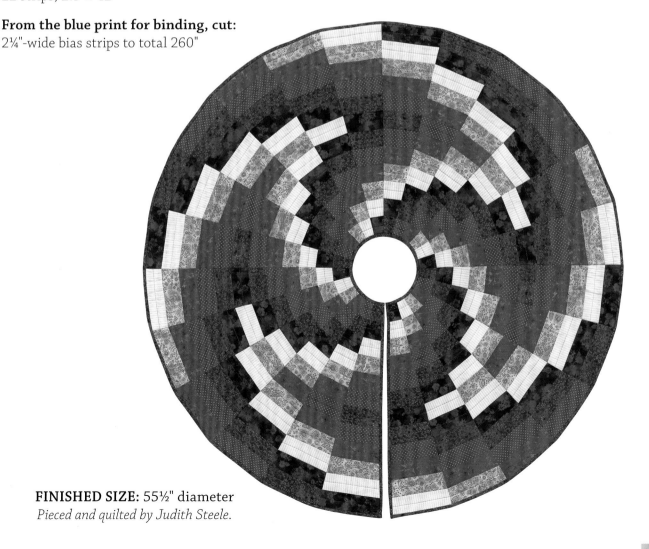

FINISHED SIZE: 55½" diameter
Pieced and quilted by Judith Steele.

each group. Arrange the strips in each group in the order shown. Sew the strips in each group together to make six strip sets that measure 24½" × 42". Using your fabric guide, compare each strip set to the diagram on page 42. The numbers assigned to your fabrics should match the number order in the diagram. Press the seam allowances in the directions indicated by the arrows.

Strip set A. Make 1.	Strip set B. Make 1.	Strip set C. Make 1.
Fabric 2	Fabric 3	Fabric 4
Fabric 3	Fabric 4	Fabric 5
Fabric 4	Fabric 5	Fabric 6
Fabric 5	Fabric 6	Fabric 1
Fabric 6	Fabric 1	Fabric 2
Fabric 1	Fabric 2	Fabric 3
Fabric 6	Fabric 1	Fabric 2
Fabric 5	Fabric 6	Fabric 1
Fabric 4	Fabric 5	Fabric 6
Fabric 3	Fabric 4	Fabric 5
Fabric 2	Fabric 3	Fabric 4
Fabric 1	Fabric 2	Fabric 3

Strip set D. Make 1.	Strip set E. Make 1.	Strip set F. Make 1.
Fabric 5	Fabric 6	Fabric 1
Fabric 6	Fabric 1	Fabric 2
Fabric 1	Fabric 2	Fabric 3
Fabric 2	Fabric 3	Fabric 4
Fabric 3	Fabric 4	Fabric 5
Fabric 4	Fabric 5	Fabric 6
Fabric 3	Fabric 4	Fabric 5
Fabric 2	Fabric 3	Fabric 4
Fabric 1	Fabric 2	Fabric 3
Fabric 6	Fabric 1	Fabric 2
Fabric 5	Fabric 6	Fabric 1
Fabric 4	Fabric 5	Fabric 6

Cutting the Wedges

Refer to "Cutting Strip Sets" on page 13 for more information as needed.

1 Trim off the selvages and straighten the left end of all the strip sets.

2 Position the wedge template on strip set A with the wide end of the template aligned with the raw edge of fabric 2 and as close to the trimmed end of the strip set as possible.

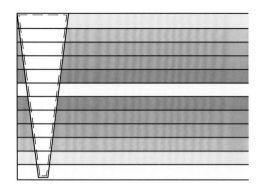

3 Trace along both edges of the template. Remove the template and then cut along the marked lines using a ruler and rotary cutter. Pin the wedge set 1 label to the wedge.

4 Rotate the template 180° and position it with the wide end along the raw edge of fabric 1. Repeat step 3 to cut the wedge, and then label it *wedge set 7*.

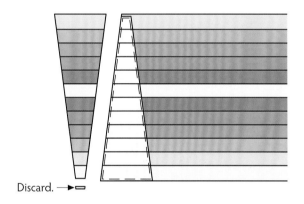

Discard.

Positioning the Wedge Template

Use the top and bottom edges of the strip set, not the previously cut angled edge, to position the wedge template correctly. You may need to cut a small sliver from the previously cut edge to position the wedge template at the correct angle.

5 Continue in this manner to cut a total of eight wedges from strip set A. Add the cut wedges to their respective stacks.

6 Repeat steps 2–5 for the remaining five strip sets, labeling wedges as follows:

Strip set B: wedge sets 2 and 8

Strip set C: wedge sets 3 and 9

Strip set D: wedge sets 4 and 10

Strip set E: wedge sets 5 and 11

Strip set F: wedge sets 6 and 12

Lock Your Seam Ends

As more wedges are added to the circle, a lot of tension is applied to the inner edge due to handling. By starting and stopping each seam on the inner edge with a backstitch or two, you can help prevent the seams from pulling apart.

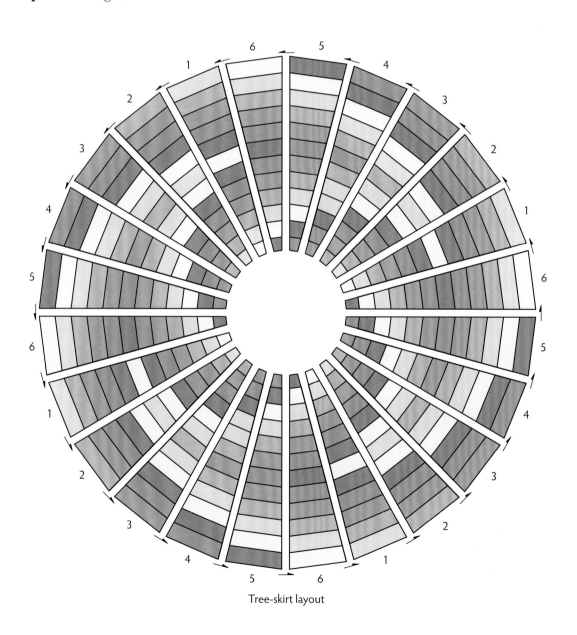

Tree-skirt layout

strip-pieced bargello

Joining the Wedges

Refer to the tree-skirt layout on page 40 and the design chart on page 42 for placement guidance throughout. Handle the wedges gently, as the edges will stretch and the seams separate easily. You'll use only wedge sets 1–6 to construct the tree skirt. Wedge sets 7–12 can be used to make a second tree skirt or the table topper (see "Variations" on page 42). Press the seam allowances in the directions indicated by the arrows.

1 Lay one segment each from wedge sets 1 and 2 side by side. Compare the wedges to the layout and the design chart. The numbers assigned to your fabrics should match the numbers in the chart. Carefully match and pin each seam intersection. Join the wedges, starting at the narrow end with a backstitch.

2 Lay one segment from wedge set 3 alongside the segment from wedge set 2. Compare the wedge to the layout and the design chart, making sure the pattern is "spinning" in the right direction. Pin and join the wedges in the same manner as before.

3 Continue adding the wedges in numerical order until all 24 wedges have been joined. Compare each wedge to the layout and the design chart, making sure the pattern is spinning in the right direction, before sewing.

Finishing the Tree Skirt

For more details on any finishing steps, go to ShopMartingale.com/HowtoQuilt to download free illustrated information.

1 Layer the tree skirt with batting and backing. Trim the excess batting and backing about 1" from the outer edges. *Do not* cut the skirt opening until the quilting has been finished. Baste the layers, and machine quilt a decorative design across the surface of the tree skirt (or take the top and backing to a professional long-arm machine quilter).

Two for One

The required strip sets yield enough segments to make two tree skirts, and each will be a little different. Or instead of making two tree skirts, you could make a tree skirt and a table topper. Each time you cut a wedge, you'll cut another one from the opposite side of the strip set. With 42"-wide fabric, you can cut eight wedges from each strip set, leaving you with four for each skirt/topper. You could even "spin" the wheels in opposite directions as I did.

Spinning Wheel Table Topper,
pieced and quilted by Judith Steele.

2 After the tree skirt is quilted, cut the skirt opening and a 7½"-diameter center circle through the backing and batting. Trim the excess batting and backing around the outer edges, even with the tree-skirt top. Trim the wedge intersections around the outer edge about ⅛", rounding them off for ease of sewing on the binding.

3 Add a label.

4 Using the blue 2¼"-wide bias strips, make the binding and attach it to the quilt.

Variations

To make a 43½"-diameter tree skirt, cut 2"-wide strips and make the center hole the same size as for the larger skirt. To make a table topper, appliqué an 8¼"-diameter circle of matching fabric in the center of the table topper before quilting it. For the tree skirt, do not cut the opening after it's quilted.

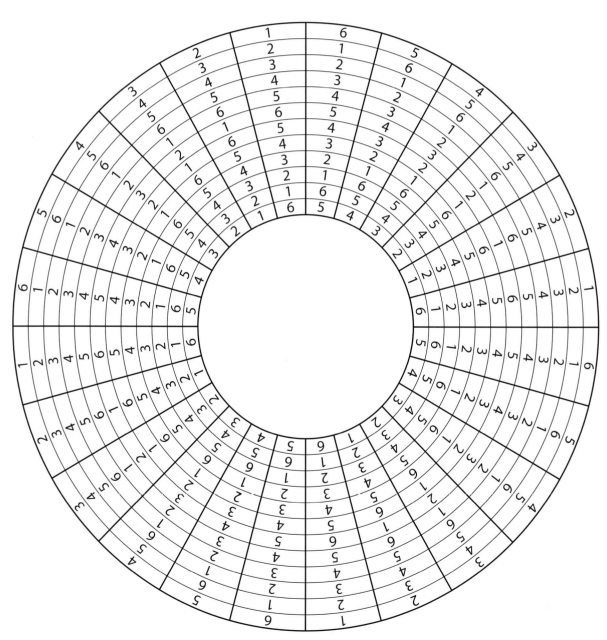

Spinning Wheel Tree Skirt design chart

strip-pieced bargello

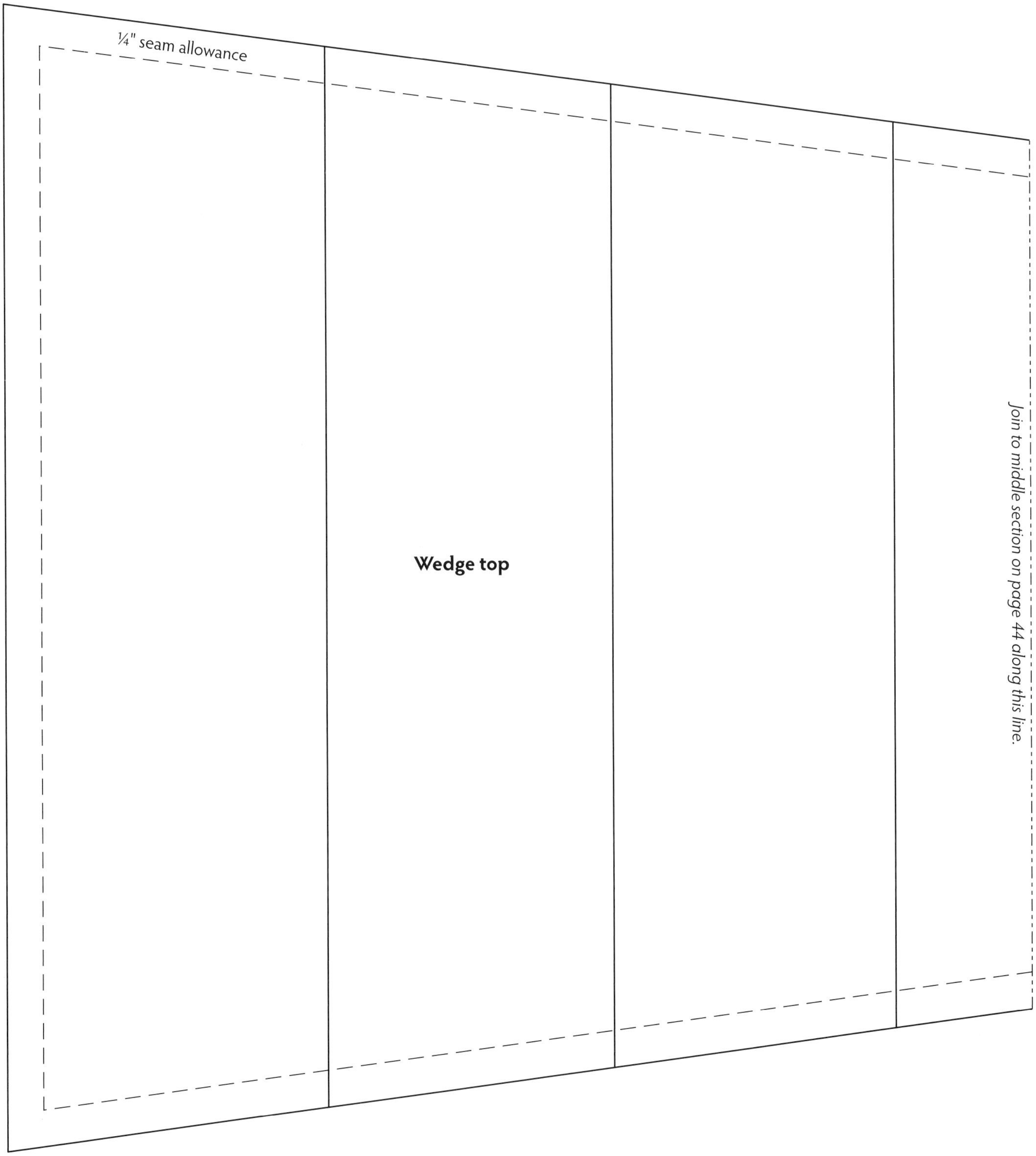

¼" seam allowance

Wedge top

Join to middle section on page 44 along this line.

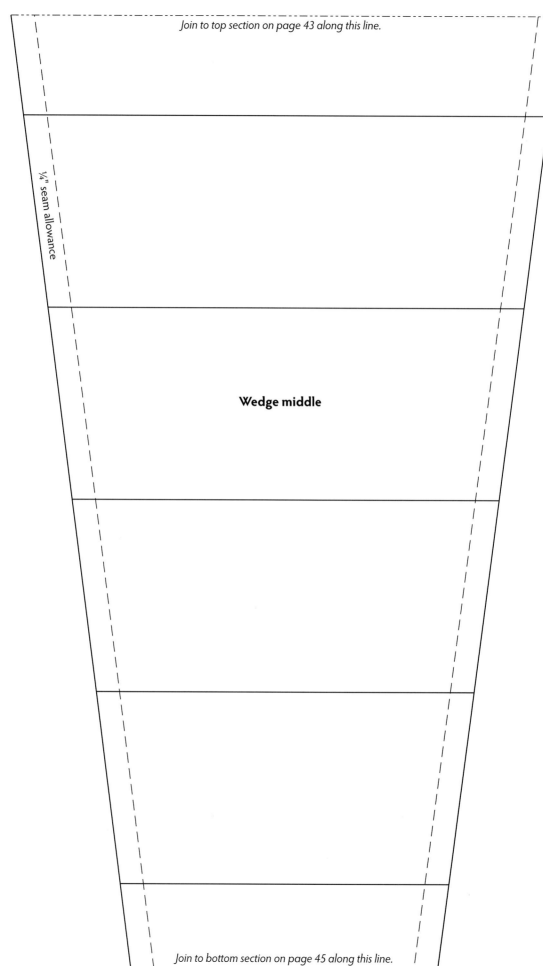

Join to top section on page 43 along this line.

¼" seam allowance

Wedge middle

Join to bottom section on page 45 along this line.

strip-pieced bargello

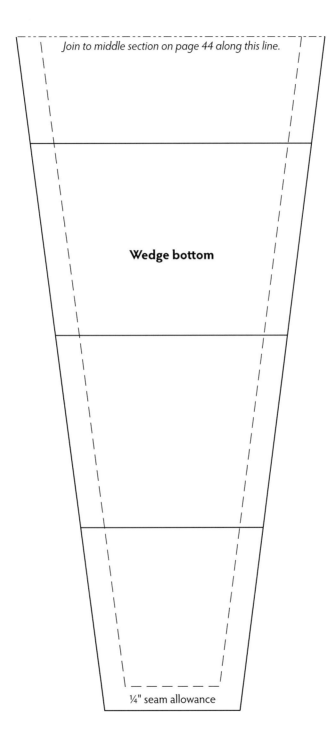

Join to middle section on page 44 along this line.

Wedge bottom

¼" seam allowance

Riding the Waves

Creating this design in teals and blues reminds me so much of an ocean wave curling over and just beginning to break. I can imagine a surfer hidden inside the barrel of the wave. So the name was obvious. The range of colors in the quilt leads me to believe that shafts of sunlight are streaming through the waves near sunset.

Fabric Selection

For this bed runner, choose 18 fabrics ranging from light greens, blues, and aquas to deep blues and teals.

Materials

Yardage is based on 42"-wide fabric.
⅓ yard *each* of 18 assorted teal, green, and blue prints for bargello (fabrics 1–18)
⅜ yard of dark blue tone on tone for border
⅝ yard of navy print for binding
3¼ yards of fabric for backing
31" × 117" piece of batting

Cutting

All measurements include ¼"-wide seam allowances.

From *each* of fabrics 1–18, cut:
4 strips, 2" × 42"

From the dark blue tone on tone, cut:
7 strips, 1½" × 42"

From the navy print, cut:
8 strips, 2¼" × 42"

Preparation

Referring to "Preparing a Fabric Guide" on page 8, assemble a fabric guide using a scrap of each of the 18 fabrics. Arrange them in order from light teal (fabric 1) to the deepest blue (fabric 18). This will ensure the fabrics are in the right order when making the strip sets.

Prepare a set of labels for columns 1–45 (*column 1, column 2,* etc.) to pin on the completed columns. Since the bed-runner top is constructed in three sections, you'll also need three additional labels (*section 1, section 2,* and *section 3*).

Making the Strip Sets

Referring to "Sewing Strip Sets" on page 10 and using the 2"-wide strips, sort the strips into four groups, with one strip of each fabric in each group. Arrange the strips in each group in

FINISHED SIZE: 24½" × 110½"
Pieced and quilted by Judith Steele.

numerical order. Sew the strips in each group together to make four strip sets that measure 27½" × 42". Press the seam allowances toward fabric 1 on two strip sets and toward fabric 18 on the remaining two strip sets.

Fabric 1		Fabric 1
Fabric 2		Fabric 2
Fabric 3		Fabric 3
Fabric 4		Fabric 4
Fabric 5		Fabric 5
Fabric 6		Fabric 6
Fabric 7		Fabric 7
Fabric 8		Fabric 8
Fabric 9		Fabric 9
Fabric 10		Fabric 10
Fabric 11		Fabric 11
Fabric 12		Fabric 12
Fabric 13		Fabric 13
Fabric 14		Fabric 14
Fabric 15		Fabric 15
Fabric 16		Fabric 16
Fabric 17		Fabric 17
Fabric 18		Fabric 18

Make 2 of each.

Making Section 1

Refer to "Cutting Strip Sets" on page 13 for more information as needed. Most of the columns are constructed with two segments. However, two columns require three segments. Before cutting any additional segments, refer to the Riding the Waves design tables on pages 52–54 and check your reserved pieces of the same width for the required fabrics.

Column 1

1 Cut two 1"-wide segments from a strip set with the seam allowances pressed toward fabric 1.

2 On the first segment, use a seam ripper to remove the stitching between fabrics 7 and 8. Reserve the 1–7 piece to use later.

3 On the second segment, sew fabric 1 to fabric 18 to make a loop. Turn the loop right side out. Use a seam ripper to remove the stitching between fabrics 8 and 9 and between fabrics 3 and 4. Reserve the 4–8 piece to use later.

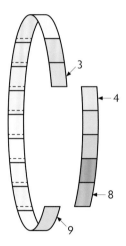

4 Sew fabric 9 on the second segment to fabric 18 on the first segment.

5 Press all the seam allowances toward the top of the column. Compare your finished column to column 1 of the design table. The numbers assigned to your fabrics should match the numbers in the table, and you should have 24 fabrics in your column. Pin the column 1 label to the top of the strip.

Column 2

1 Cut two 1¼"-wide strips from a strip set with the seam allowances pressed toward fabric 18.

2 On the first segment, use a seam ripper to remove the stitching between fabrics 2 and 3 and between fabrics 6 and 7. Save the two-piece segment for step 5. Reserve the 3–6 piece to use later.

3 On the second segment, sew fabric 1 to fabric 18 to make a loop. Turn the loop right side out. Use a seam ripper to remove the stitching between fabrics 2 and 3 and between fabrics 10 and 11. Reserve the 3–10 piece to use later.

4 Sew fabric 18 on the first segment to fabric 11 on the second segment. Fabric 7 will now be at the top of the column.

5 Sew fabric 1 on the two-piece segment from step 2 to fabric 2 at the bottom of the column.

6 Press all the seam allowances toward the bottom of the column. Compare your finished column to column 2 of the design table. The numbers assigned to your fabrics should match the numbers in the table, and you should have 24 fabrics in your column. Pin the column 2 label to the top of the strip.

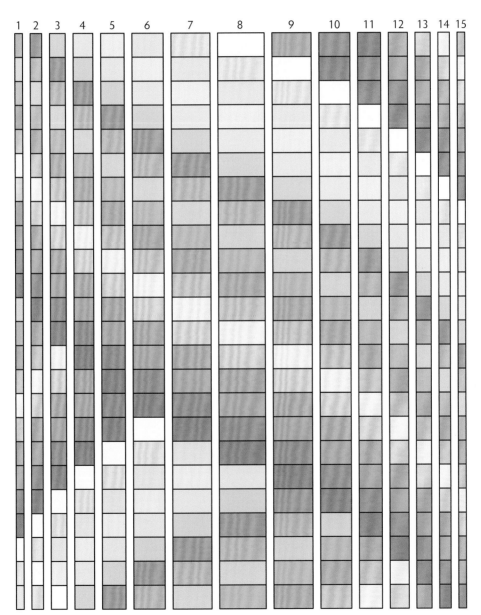

Bed-runner layout
Section 1

Working from the Design Table

1 Continue working in the same manner indicated in the design table for section 1, cutting two segments for each column in the widths indicated in the design table. When constructing columns 11 and 13 (and columns 26, 27, and 41–44 for sections 2 and 3), cut three segments in the widths indicated *OR* you may be able to utilize some of the reserved sections that are the correct width. Referring to your fabric guide and using the bold lines on the design table as a reference, remove the stitching between fabrics, as needed, and join the segments in the order indicated for the column you are making.

2 After completing each new column, compare it to the design table to make sure the fabric numbers and pressing direction are accurate. Then pin the appropriate label to the top of the column.

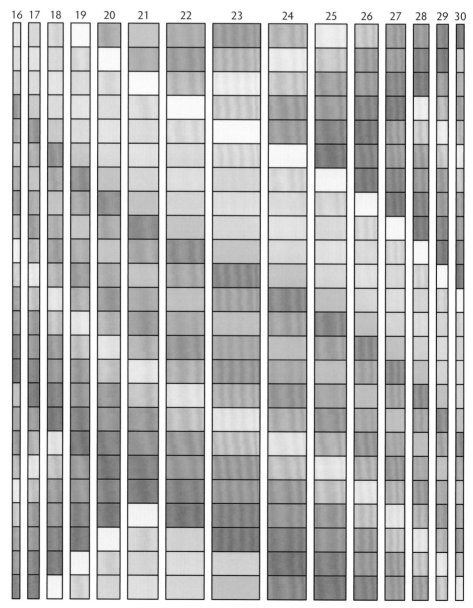

Bed-runner layout
Section 2

strip-pieced bargello

Making Section 1

1 With right sides together and starting with columns 1 and 2, join the columns in pairs, sewing along their long edges and carefully matching the seam intersections. Press the seam allowances toward the odd-numbered columns.

2 Join the pairs and press the seam allowances toward the lower-numbered columns.

3 Continue in this manner until all the columns in section 1 have been joined.

4 Verify that the section matches the design table, and then pin the section 1 label to the top of the section.

Making Sections 2 and 3

Construct the columns for sections 2 and 3 in the same manner as for section 1, checking the reserved pieces of the same width for the correct fabrics before cutting additional segments for each new column. When joining the columns for

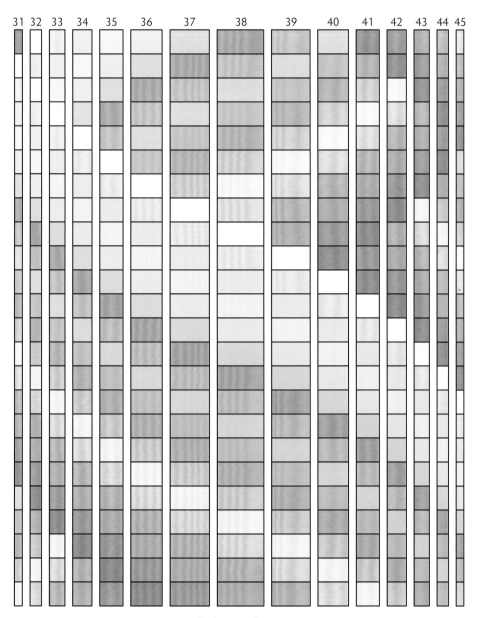

Bed-runner layout
Section 3

section 2, press the seam allowances toward the higher-numbered columns. For section 3, press the seam allowances toward the lower-numbered columns.

Assembling the Bed Runner

1 Join section 1 to section 2, matching the seam intersections. Compare the sections to the photo on page 47. Press the seam allowances in one direction.

2 Sew section 3 to the bottom of section 2. Press the seam allowances in one direction. The bed-runner top should measure 22½" × 108½", including seam allowances.

3 Join the dark blue 1½"-wide strips end to end. From the pieced strip, cut two 108½"-long strips and sew them to the long sides of the bed runner. From the remaining pieced strip, cut two 24½"-long strips and sew them to the ends of the bed runner. Press all seam allowances toward the dark blue strips. The bed runner should now measure 24½" × 110½".

Design Table: Riding the Waves

SECTION 1															
Column	1	2	3	4	5	6	7	8	9	10	11	12	13	14	15
Cut width of segments	1"	1¼"	1½"	1¾"	2"	2½"	3"	3½"	3"	2½"	2"	1¾"	1½"	1¼"	1"
Pressing direction	↑	↓	↑	↓	↑	↓	↑	↓	↑	↓	↑	↓	↑	↓	↑
Number of segments to cut	2	2	2	2	2	2	2	2	2	2	3	2	3	2	2
Fabric number	8	7	6	5	4	3	2	1	16	17	18	15	14	13	12
	9	8	7	6	5	4	3	2	1	18	17	16	15	14	13
	10	9	8	7	6	5	4	3	2	1	18	17	16	15	14
	11	10	9	8	7	6	5	4	3	2	1	18	17	16	15
	12	11	10	9	8	7	6	5	4	3	2	1	18	17	16
	13	12	11	10	9	8	7	6	5	4	3	2	1	18	17
	14	13	12	11	10	9	8	7	6	5	4	3	2	1	18
	15	14	13	12	11	10	9	8	7	6	5	4	3	2	1
	16	15	14	13	12	11	10	9	8	7	6	5	4	3	2
	17	16	15	14	13	12	11	10	9	8	7	6	5	4	3
	18	17	16	15	14	13	12	11	10	9	8	7	6	5	4
	9	18	17	16	15	14	13	12	11	10	9	8	7	6	5
	10	11	18	17	16	15	14	13	12	11	10	9	8	7	6
	11	12	13	18	17	16	15	14	13	12	11	10	9	8	7
	12	13	14	15	18	17	16	15	14	13	12	11	10	9	8
	13	14	15	16	17	18	17	16	15	14	13	12	11	10	9
	14	15	16	17	18	1	18	17	16	15	14	13	12	11	10
	15	16	17	18	1	2	3	18	17	16	15	14	13	12	11
	16	17	18	1	2	3	4	5	18	17	16	15	14	13	12
	17	18	1	2	3	4	5	6	7	18	17	16	15	14	13
	18	1	2	3	4	5	6	7	8	9	18	17	16	15	14
	1	2	3	4	5	6	7	8	9	10	11	18	17	16	15
	2	1	4	5	6	7	8	9	10	11	12	13	18	17	16
	3	2	1	6	7	8	9	10	11	12	13	14	15	18	17

Finishing the Bed Runner

For more details on any finishing steps, go to ShopMartingale.com/HowtoQuilt to download free illustrated information.

1 Layer the bed-runner top with batting and backing; baste. Machine quilt a decorative design across the surface of the bed runner (or take the top and backing to a professional long-arm machine quilter).

2 Add a label.

3 Using the navy 2¼"-wide strips, make the binding and attach it to the bed runner.

SECTION 2															
Column	16	17	18	19	20	21	22	23	24	25	26	27	28	29	30
Cut width of segments	1"	1¼"	1½"	1¾"	2"	2½"	3"	3½"	3"	2½"	2"	1¾"	1½"	1¼"	1"
Pressing direction	↑	↓	↑	↓	↑	↓	↑	↓	↑	↓	↑	↓	↑	↓	↑
Number of segments to cut	2	2	2	2	2	2	2	2	2	2	3	3	2	2	2
Fabric number	4	3	2	1	8	9	10	11	12	13	14	15	16	17	18
	5	4	3	2	1	10	11	12	13	14	15	16	17	18	9
	6	5	4	3	2	1	12	13	14	15	16	17	18	11	10
	7	6	5	4	3	2	1	14	15	16	17	18	13	12	11
	8	7	6	5	4	3	2	1	16	17	18	15	14	13	12
	9	8	7	6	5	4	3	2	1	18	17	16	15	14	13
	10	9	8	7	6	5	4	3	2	1	18	17	16	15	14
	11	10	9	8	7	6	5	4	3	2	1	18	17	16	15
	12	11	10	9	8	7	6	5	4	3	2	1	18	17	16
	13	12	11	10	9	8	7	6	5	4	3	2	1	18	17
	14	13	12	11	10	9	8	7	6	5	4	3	2	1	18
	15	14	13	12	11	10	9	8	7	6	5	4	3	2	1
	16	15	14	13	12	11	10	9	8	7	6	5	4	3	2
	17	16	15	14	13	12	11	10	9	8	7	6	5	4	3
	18	17	16	15	14	13	12	11	10	9	8	7	6	5	4
	9	18	17	16	15	14	13	12	11	10	9	8	7	6	5
	10	11	18	17	16	15	14	13	12	11	10	9	8	7	6
	11	12	13	18	17	16	15	14	13	12	11	10	9	8	7
	12	13	14	15	18	17	16	15	14	13	12	11	10	9	8
	13	14	15	16	17	18	17	16	15	14	13	12	11	10	9
	14	15	16	17	18	1	18	17	16	15	14	13	12	11	10
	15	16	17	18	1	2	3	18	17	16	15	14	13	12	11
	16	17	18	1	2	3	4	5	18	17	16	15	14	13	12
	17	18	1	2	3	4	5	6	7	18	17	16	15	14	13

SECTION 3

Column	31	32	33	34	35	36	37	38	39	40	41	42	43	44	45
Cut width of segments	1"	1¼"	1½"	1¾"	2"	2½"	3"	3½"	3"	2½"	2"	1¾"	1½"	1¼"	1"
Pressing direction	↑	↓	↑	↓	↑	↓	↑	↓	↑	↓	↑	↓	↑	↓	↑
Number of segments to cut	2	2	2	2	2	2	2	2	2	2	3	3	3	3	2
Fabric number	18	1	2	3	4	5	6	7	8	9	18	17	16	15	14
	1	2	3	4	5	6	7	8	9	10	11	18	17	16	15
	2	1	4	5	6	7	8	9	10	11	12	13	18	17	16
	3	2	1	6	7	8	9	10	11	12	13	14	15	18	17
	4	3	2	1	8	9	10	11	12	13	14	15	16	17	18
	5	4	3	2	1	10	11	12	13	14	15	16	17	18	9
	6	5	4	3	2	1	12	13	14	15	16	17	18	11	10
	7	6	5	4	3	2	1	14	15	16	17	18	13	12	11
	8	7	6	5	4	3	2	1	16	17	18	15	14	13	12
	9	8	7	6	5	4	3	2	1	18	17	16	15	14	13
	10	9	8	7	6	5	4	3	2	1	18	17	16	15	14
	11	10	9	8	7	6	5	4	3	2	1	18	17	16	15
	12	11	10	9	8	7	6	5	4	3	2	1	18	17	16
	13	12	11	10	9	8	7	6	5	4	3	2	1	18	17
	14	13	12	11	10	9	8	7	6	5	4	3	2	1	18
	15	14	13	12	11	10	9	8	7	6	5	4	3	2	1
	16	15	14	13	12	11	10	9	8	7	6	5	4	3	2
	17	16	15	14	13	12	11	10	9	8	7	6	5	4	3
	18	17	16	15	14	13	12	11	10	9	8	7	6	5	4
	9	18	17	16	15	14	13	12	11	10	9	8	7	6	5
	10	11	18	17	16	15	14	13	12	11	10	9	8	7	6
	11	12	13	18	17	16	15	14	13	12	11	10	9	8	7
	12	13	14	15	18	17	16	15	14	13	12	11	10	9	8
	13	14	15	16	17	18	17	16	15	14	13	12	11	10	9

strip-pieced bargello

Down the Bannister

My older daughter adores purple, so I just had to include a quilt in her favorite color. I love the way the colors seem to swirl and swish downward from the top-left corner to the bottom right. The shape brought to mind a staircase in a stately house and—rebel that I am—how much fun it would be to slide down the highly polished handrail. Making the quilt was fun, too, because I constructed bargello columns of the same width at the same time, working from the outer quilt edges in toward the center. This approach saved a lot of fabric, with the added bonus of fewer segments to cut from the strip sets.

Fabric Selection

The 18 fabrics in this quilt range from maroon to hot pink, and from mauve to deep purple.

Materials

Yardage is based on 42"-wide fabric.
⅓ yard *each* of 18 assorted maroon to dark purple fabrics for bargello (fabrics 1–18)
½ yard of purple print for border
½ yard of dark purple print for binding
2⅝ yards of fabric for backing
46" × 80" piece of batting

Cutting

All measurements include ¼"-wide seam allowances.

From *each* of fabrics 1–18, cut:
4 strips, 2" × 42"

From the purple print, cut:
6 strips, 2½" × 42"

From the dark purple print, cut:
6 strips, 2¼" × 42"

Preparation

Referring to "Preparing a Fabric Guide" on page 8, assemble a fabric guide using a scrap of each of the 18 fabrics. Arrange them in order from maroon (fabric 1) to deep purple (fabric 18). This will ensure the fabrics are in the right order when making the strip sets.

Prepare a set of labels for columns 1–21 (*column 1, column 2,* etc.) to pin on the completed columns.

Making the Strip Sets

Referring to "Sewing Strip Sets" on page 10 and using the 2"-wide strips, sort the strips into four groups, with one strip of each fabric in each group. Arrange the strips in each group in numerical order. Sew the strips in each group

together to make four strip sets that measure 27½" × 42". Press the seam allowances toward fabric 1 on two strip sets and toward fabric 18 on the remaining two strip sets.

Make 2 of each.

Making Columns 1 and 21

Refer to "Cutting Strip Sets" on page 13 for more information as needed. Keep in mind that you'll be making columns for opposite sides of the quilt at the same time, gradually working inward.

1 Cut seven 1"-wide segments from a strip set with the seam allowances pressed toward fabric 1.

2 On the first segment, use a seam ripper to remove the stitching between fabrics 2 and 3 and between fabrics 14 and 15. Discard the 3–14 piece and reserve the two-fabric piece to use in step 6.

3 Sew fabric 18 on the first segment to fabric 1 on the second segment. Fabric 18 will be at the bottom of the column.

4 On a third segment, use a seam ripper to remove the stitching between fabrics 14 and 15. Reserve the 1–14 piece to use for column 21. Sew fabric 15 on the third segment to fabric 18 at the bottom of the column.

5 Sew fabric 1 on a fourth segment to fabric 18 at the bottom of the column.

FINISHED SIZE: 40" × 73½"
Pieced by Judith Steele; quilted by Trish Ryan.

6 Sew fabric 1 on the two-fabric piece from step 2 to fabric 18 at the bottom of the column. Press all the seam allowances toward the top of the column. Compare your finished column to column 1 of the Down the Bannister design tables on pages 61 and 62. The numbers assigned to your fabrics should match the numbers in the table, and you should have 46 fabrics in your column. Pin the column 1 label to the top of the finished column.

7 On the fifth segment, use a seam ripper to remove the stitching between fabrics 4 and 5 and between fabrics 16 and 17. Discard the 5–16 piece and reserve the 1–4 piece to use in step 9.

8 Sew fabric 18 on the fifth segment to fabric 1 on the sixth segment. Fabric 18 will be at the bottom of the column.

9 Sew fabric 1 on the 1–4 piece reserved in step 7 to fabric 18 at the bottom of the column. Fabric 4 will now be at the bottom of the column.

10 Sew fabric 1 on the seventh segment to fabric 4 at the bottom of the column. Fabric 18 will now be at the bottom of the column.

11 On the 1–14 piece reserved in step 4, use a seam ripper to remove the stitching between fabrics 4 and 5. Discard the 5–14 piece.

12 Sew fabric 1 on the reserved piece to fabric 18 at the bottom of the column. Press all seam allowances toward the top of the column. Compare your finished column to column 21 of the design table. The numbers assigned to your fabrics should match the numbers in the table, and you should have 46 fabrics in your column. Pin the column 21 label to the top of the finished column.

Making Columns 2 and 20

1 Cut eight 1¼"-wide segments from a strip set with seam allowances pressed toward fabric 18.

2 On the first segment, sew fabric 1 to fabric 18 to make a loop.

3 Turn the loop right side out. Use a seam ripper to remove the stitching between fabrics

2 and 3 and between fabrics 15 and 16. Discard the 3–15 piece. Fabric 2 will be at the bottom of the column.

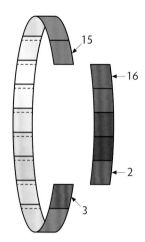

4 Sew fabric 1 on a second segment to fabric 2 at the bottom of the column. Fabric 18 will be at the bottom of the column.

5 On a third segment, use a seam ripper to remove the stitching between fabrics 3 and 4 and between fabrics 16 and 17. Discard the 4–16 piece and reserve the 1–3 piece to use in step 7.

6 Using the two-fabric piece from step 5, sew fabric 17 to fabric 18 at the bottom of the column. Sew fabric 1 on the fourth segment to fabric 18 at the bottom of the column.

7 Sew fabric 1 on the three-fabric piece from step 5 to fabric 18 to complete the column. Press all the seam allowances toward the bottom of the column. Compare your finished column to column 2 of the design table. The numbers assigned to your fabrics should match the numbers in the table, and you should have 46 fabrics in your column. Pin the column 2 label to the top of the finished column.

8 On a fifth segment, use a seam ripper to remove the stitching between fabrics 2 and 3 and between fabrics 15 and 16. Discard the 3–15 piece.

9 Sew fabric 18 on the three-fabric piece to fabric 1 on a sixth segment. Then sew fabric 1 on the two-fabric piece to fabric 18. Fabric 2 will be at the bottom of the column.

10 Sew fabric 1 on a seventh segment to fabric 2 at the bottom of the column.

11 On the eighth segment, sew fabric 1 to fabric 18 to make a loop. Turn the loop right side out. Use a seam ripper to remove the stitching between fabrics 3 and 4 and between fabrics 16 and 17. Discard the 4–16 piece.

12 Sew fabric 17 to fabric 18 at the bottom of the column. Press all seam allowances toward the bottom of the column. Compare your finished column to column 20 of the design table. The numbers assigned to your fabrics should match the numbers in the table, and you should have 46 fabrics in your column. Pin the column 20 label to the top of the finished strip.

Working from the Design Table

1 Continue working in the same manner, cutting the number of segments in the width indicated in the design table, and then using those segments to make a same-width column for the opposite side of the quilt. Referring to your fabric guide and using the bold lines on the table as a reference, remove the stitching between fabrics, as needed, and join the segments in the order indicated for the column you are making.

2 After completing each new column, compare it to the design table to make sure the fabric numbers and pressing direction are accurate. Then pin the appropriate label to the top of the column.

Assembling the Quilt Top

1 With right sides together and starting with columns 1 and 2, join the columns in pairs, sewing along their long edges and carefully matching the seam intersections. Press the seam allowances toward the odd-numbered columns.

2 Join the pairs and press the seam allowances toward the lower-numbered columns.

3 Continue in this manner until all the columns have been joined. The quilt top should measure 36" × 69½", including the seam allowances.

4 Join the purple print 2½"-wide strips end to end. From the pieced strip, cut two 69½"-long strips and sew them to the long sides of the quilt top. From the remaining pieced strip, cut two 40"-long strips and sew them to the top and bottom of the quilt top. Press all seam allowances toward the purple strips. The quilt top should now measure 40" × 73½".

Finishing the Quilt

For more details on any finishing steps, go to ShopMartingale.com/HowtoQuilt to download free illustrated information.

1 Layer the quilt top with batting and backing; baste. Machine quilt a decorative design across the quilt surface (or take the top and backing to a professional long-arm machine quilter).

2 Add a label.

3 Using the dark purple 2¼"-wide strips, make the binding and attach it to the quilt.

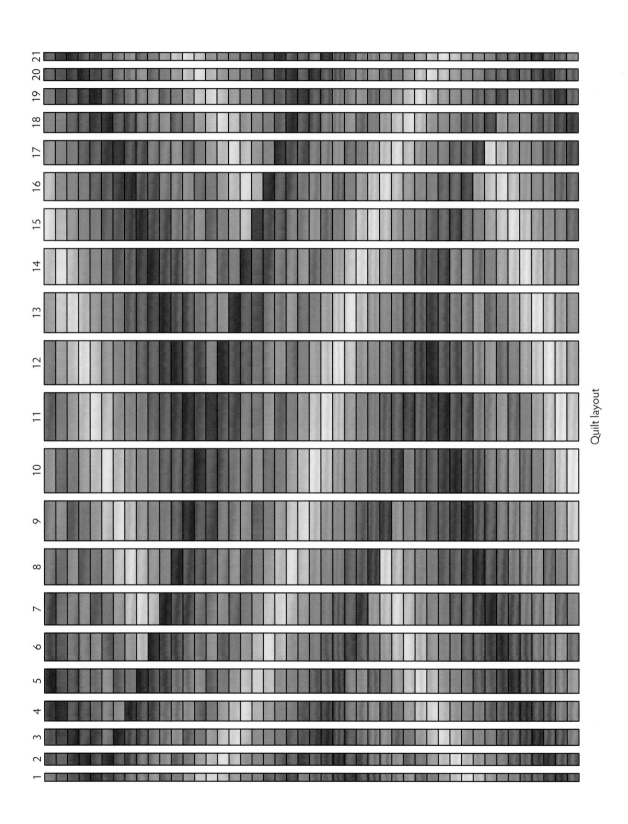

Quilt layout

strip-pieced bargello

Design Table: Down the Bannister

Column	1	2	3	4	5	6	7	8	9	10	11
Cut width of segments	1"	1¼"	1½"	1¾"	2"	2¼"	2½"	2¾"	3"	3¼"	3½"
Pressing direction	↑	↓	↑	↓	↑	↓	↑	↓	↑	↓	↑
Number of segments to cut	7	8	7	6	6	6	6	6	6	6	3
Fabric number	15	16	17	18	1	2	3	4	5	6	7
	16	17	18	1	2	3	4	5	6	7	8
	17	18	1	2	3	4	5	6	7	8	9
	18	1	2	3	4	5	6	7	8	9	10
	1	2	3	4	5	6	7	8	9	10	11
	2	1	4	5	6	7	8	9	10	11	12
	3	2	1	6	7	8	9	10	11	12	13
	4	3	2	1	8	9	10	11	12	13	14
	5	4	3	2	1	10	11	12	13	14	15
	6	5	4	3	2	1	12	13	14	15	16
	7	6	5	4	3	2	1	14	15	16	17
	8	7	6	5	4	3	2	1	16	17	18
	9	8	7	6	5	4	3	2	1	18	1
	10	9	8	7	6	5	4	3	2	1	2
	11	10	9	8	7	6	5	4	3	2	1
	12	11	10	9	8	7	6	5	4	3	2
	13	12	11	10	9	8	7	6	5	4	3
	14	13	12	11	10	9	8	7	6	5	4
	15	14	13	12	11	10	9	8	7	6	5
	16	15	14	13	12	11	10	9	8	7	6
	17	16	15	14	13	12	11	10	9	8	7
	18	17	16	15	14	13	12	11	10	9	8
	15	18	17	16	15	14	13	12	11	10	9
	16	17	18	17	16	15	14	13	12	11	10
	17	18	1	18	17	16	15	14	13	12	11
	18	1	2	3	18	17	16	15	14	13	12
	1	2	3	4	5	18	17	16	15	14	13
	2	3	4	5	6	7	18	17	16	15	14
	3	4	5	6	7	8	9	18	17	16	15
	4	5	6	7	8	9	10	11	18	17	16
	5	6	7	8	9	10	11	12	13	18	17
	6	7	8	9	10	11	12	13	14	15	18
	7	8	9	10	11	12	13	14	15	16	17
	8	9	10	11	12	13	14	15	16	17	18
	9	10	11	12	13	14	15	16	17	18	1
	10	11	12	13	14	15	16	17	18	1	2
	11	12	13	14	15	16	17	18	1	2	3
	12	13	14	15	16	17	18	1	2	3	4
	13	14	15	16	17	18	1	2	3	4	5
	14	15	16	17	18	1	2	3	4	5	6
	15	16	17	18	1	2	3	4	5	6	7
	16	17	18	1	2	3	4	5	6	7	8
	17	18	1	2	3	4	5	6	7	8	9
	18	1	2	3	4	5	6	7	8	9	10
	1	2	3	4	5	6	7	8	9	10	11
	2	3	4	5	6	7	8	9	10	11	12

Column	12	13	14	15	16	17	18	19	20	21
Cut width of segments	3¼"	3"	2¾"	2½"	2¼"	2"	1¾"	1½"	1¼"	1"
Pressing direction	↓	↑	↓	↑	↓	↑	↓	↑	↓	↑
Fabric number	8	9	10	11	12	13	14	15	16	17
	9	10	11	12	13	14	15	16	17	18
	10	11	12	13	14	15	16	17	18	1
	11	12	13	14	15	16	17	18	1	2
	12	13	14	15	16	17	18	1	2	3
	13	14	15	16	17	18	1	2	3	4
	14	15	16	17	18	1	2	3	4	5
	15	16	17	18	1	2	3	4	5	6
	16	17	18	1	2	3	4	5	6	7
	17	18	1	2	3	4	5	6	7	8
	18	1	2	3	4	5	6	7	8	9
	1	2	3	4	5	6	7	8	9	10
	2	3	4	5	6	7	8	9	10	11
	3	4	5	6	7	8	9	10	11	12
	4	5	6	7	8	9	10	11	12	13
	1	6	7	8	9	10	11	12	13	14
	2	1	8	9	10	11	12	13	14	15
	3	2	1	10	11	12	13	14	15	16
	4	3	2	1	12	13	14	15	16	17
	5	4	3	2	1	14	15	16	17	18
	6	5	4	3	2	1	16	17	18	1
	7	6	5	4	3	2	1	18	1	2
	8	7	6	5	4	3	2	1	2	3
	9	8	7	6	5	4	3	2	1	4
	10	9	8	7	6	5	4	3	2	1
	11	10	9	8	7	6	5	4	3	2
	12	11	10	9	8	7	6	5	4	3
	13	12	11	10	9	8	7	6	5	4
	14	13	12	11	10	9	8	7	6	5
	15	14	13	12	11	10	9	8	7	6
	16	15	14	13	12	11	10	9	8	7
	17	16	15	14	13	12	11	10	9	8
	18	17	16	15	14	13	12	11	10	9
	1	18	17	16	15	14	13	12	11	10
	2	3	18	17	16	15	14	13	12	11
	3	4	5	18	17	16	15	14	13	12
	4	5	6	7	18	17	16	15	14	13
	5	6	7	8	9	18	17	16	15	14
	6	7	8	9	10	11	18	17	16	15
	7	8	9	10	11	12	13	18	17	16
	8	9	10	11	12	13	14	15	18	17
	9	10	11	12	13	14	15	16	17	18
	10	11	12	13	14	15	16	17	18	1
	11	12	13	14	15	16	17	18	1	2
	12	13	14	15	16	17	18	1	2	3
	13	14	15	16	17	18	1	2	3	4

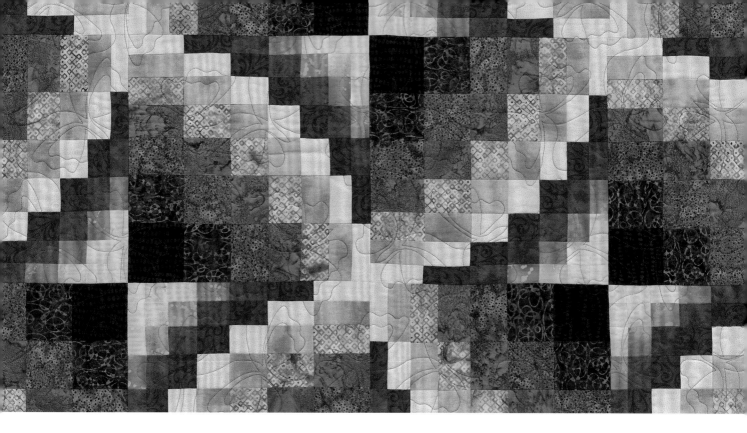

Dancing Butterflies

Using shorter columns and assembling them into blocks introduces the potential for many new bargello effects. Experimenting with layouts, I was struck by how this design strongly reminded me of butterflies fluttering this way and that. The way the bright butterfly wings contrast against the darker background makes them pop out for a dramatic 3-D effect, which is one of the things I love in bargello quilts.

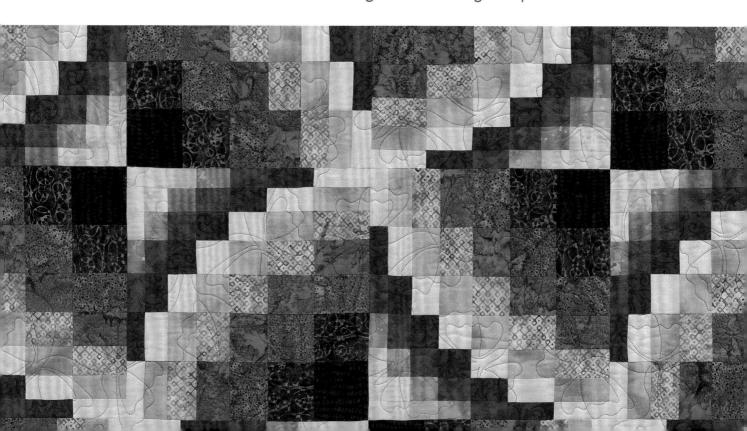

Fabric Selection

Look for 13 fabrics in two color groups: one group made up of six yellow to red fabrics, and a second group made up of seven fabrics in beige to black. Fabrics in each color group should range from light to dark.

Materials

Yardage is based on 42"-wide fabric.

⅛ yard of yellow tone on tone for bargello (fabric 1)

¼ yard of dark yellow tone on tone for bargello (fabric 2)

⅜ yard of light orange tone on tone for bargello (fabric 3)

⅝ yard of dark orange tone on tone for bargello (fabric 4)

¾ yard of red print for bargello (fabric 5)

1½ yards of dark red print for bargello and inner border (fabric 6)

1⅓ yards of beige print for bargello (fabric 7)

1⅓ yards of gray tone on tone for bargello (fabric 8)

1¼ yards of light green tone on tone for bargello (fabric 9)

1⅛ yards of green tone on tone for bargello (fabric 10)

1 yard of dark gray tone on tone for bargello (fabric 11)

¾ yard of charcoal print for bargello (fabric 12)

½ yard of black print for bargello (fabric 13)

⅝ yard of brown print for outer border

⅔ yard of dark brown print for binding

7¾ yards of fabric for backing

93" × 93" square of batting

Cutting

All measurements include ¼"-wide seam allowances. As you cut the strips, sort them into their respective strip sets (A, B, C, and so on).

From fabric 1, cut:
2 strips, 1½" × 42" (A)

From fabric 2, cut:
2 strips, 1¾" × 42" (A)
2 strips, 1½" × 42" (B)

From fabric 3, cut:
2 strips, 2" × 42" (A)
2 strips, 1¾" × 42" (B)
2 strips, 1½" × 42" (C)

From fabric 4, cut:
2 strips, 2¼" × 42" (A)
2 strips, 2" × 42" (B)
2 strips, 1¾" × 42" (C)
3 strips, 1½" × 42" (D)

From fabric 5, cut:
2 strips, 2½" × 42" (A)
2 strips, 2¼" × 42" (B)
2 strips, 2" × 42" (C)
3 strips, 1¾" × 42" (D)
3 strips, 1½" × 42" (E)

From fabric 6, cut:
2 strips, 3" × 42" (A)
2 strips, 2½" × 42" (B)
2 strips, 2¼" × 42" (C)
12 strips, 2" × 42" (D; set aside 9 for inner border)
3 strips, 1¾" × 42" (E)
3 strips, 1½" × 42" (F)

From fabric 7, cut:
2 strips, 3½" × 42" (A)
2 strips, 3" × 42" (B)
2 strips, 2½" × 42" (C)
3 strips, 2¼" × 42" (D)
3 strips, 2" × 42" (E)
3 strips, 1¾" × 42" (F)
4 strips, 1½" × 42" (G)

Continued on page 66

FINISHED QUILT SIZE: 84½" × 84½"
FINISHED BLOCK SIZE: 13" × 13"
Pieced by Judith Steele; quilted by Trish Ryan.

Continued from page 64

From fabric 8, cut:
2 strips, 3½" × 42" (B)
2 strips, 3" × 42" (C)
3 strips, 2½" × 42" (D)
3 strips, 2¼" × 42" (E)
3 strips, 2" × 42" (F)
4 strips, 1¾" × 42" (G)

From fabric 9, cut:
2 strips, 3½" × 42" (C)
3 strips, 3" × 42" (D)
3 strips, 2½" × 42" (E)
3 strips, 2¼" × 42" (F)
4 strips, 2" × 42" (G)

From fabric 10, cut:
3 strips, 3½" × 42" (D)
3 strips, 3" × 42" (E)
3 strips, 2½" × 42" (F)
4 strips, 2¼" × 42" (G)

From fabric 11, cut:
3 strips, 3½" × 42" (E)
3 strips, 3" × 42" (F)
4 strips, 2½" × 42" (G)

From fabric 12, cut:
3 strips, 3½" × 42" (F)
4 strips, 3" × 42" (G)

From fabric 13, cut:
4 strips, 3½" × 42" (G)

From the brown print, cut:
9 strips, 2" × 42"

From the dark brown print, cut:
9 strips, 2¼" × 42"

Preparation

Referring to "Preparing a Fabric Guide" on page 8, assemble a fabric guide using a scrap of each of the 13 fabrics. Arrange them in order from yellow (fabric 1) to black (fabric 13). This will ensure that the fabrics are in the right order when making the strip sets.

Prepare a set of labels for strip sets A–G (*strip set A*, *strip set B*, etc.) to pin on the completed strip sets.

Making the Strip Sets

Refer to "Sewing Strip Sets" on page 10 as needed. Press the seam allowances in the directions indicated by the arrows.

Strip Set A

1 Sort the A strips into two groups, with one strip of each fabric in each group. Sew the strips in each group together to make two strip sets. The strip sets should measure 13½" × 42".

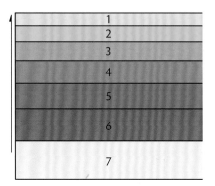

Strip set A.
Make 2.

2 Cut the strip sets into 36 segments, 1½" × 13½", stacking them neatly together. Pin the strip set A label to the top of the stack.

Strip Set B

1 Sort the B strips into two groups, with one strip of each fabric in each group. Sew the strips in each group together to make two strip sets. The strip sets should measure 13½" × 42".

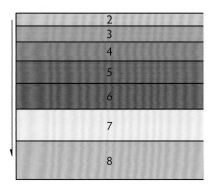

Strip set B.
Make 2.

2 Cut the strip sets into 36 segments, 1¾" × 13½", stacking them neatly together. Pin the strip set B label to the top of the stack.

Strip Set C

1 Sort the C strips into two groups, with one strip of each fabric in each group. Sew the strips in each group together to make two strip sets. The strip sets should measure 13½" × 42".

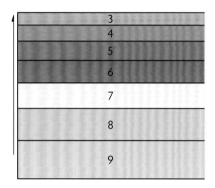

Strip set C.
Make 2.

2 Cut the strip sets into 36 segments, 2" × 13½", stacking them neatly together. Pin the strip set C label to the top of the stack.

Strip Set D

1 Sort the D strips into three groups, with one strip of each fabric in each group. Sew the strips in each group together to make three strip sets. The strip sets should measure 13½" × 42".

Strip set D.
Make 3.

2 Cut the strip sets into 36 segments, 2¼" × 13½", stacking them neatly together. Pin the strip set D label to the top of the stack.

Strip Set E

1 Sort the E strips into three groups, with one strip of each fabric in each group. Sew the strips in each group together to make three strip sets. The strip sets should measure 13½" × 42".

Strip set E.
Make 3.

2 Cut the strip sets into 36 segments, 2½" × 13½", stacking them neatly together. Pin the strip set E label to the top of the stack.

Strip Set F

1 Sort the F strips into three groups, with one strip of each fabric in each group. Sew the strips in each group together to make three strip sets. The strip sets should measure 13½" × 42".

Strip set F.
Make 3.

2 Cut the strip sets into 36 segments, 3" × 13½", stacking them neatly together. Pin the strip set F label to the top of the stack.

Strip Set G

1 Sort the G strips into four groups, with one strip of each fabric in each group. Sew the strips in each group together to make four strip sets. The strip sets should measure 13½" × 42".

| 7 |
| 8 |
| 9 |
| 10 |
| 11 |
| 12 |
| 13 |

Strip set G.
Make 4.

2 Cut the strip sets into 36 segments, 3½" × 13½", stacking them neatly together. Pin the strip set G label to the top of the stack.

Extra Strip Set

If your fabrics are 42" wide after washing and trimming off the selvages, you may need to make only three G strip sets. Wait to make the fourth strip set until you see how many segments you can cut from the first three G strip sets.

Making the Blocks

Lay out one segment from each of the A–G strip sets. Join the segments, carefully matching the seam intersections, to make a block that measures 13½" square, including the seam allowances. Make 36 blocks.

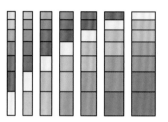

Make 36 blocks,
13½" × 13½".

Assembling the Quilt Top

1 Lay out the blocks in six rows of six blocks each, rotating the blocks in each row and from row to row as shown in the quilt layout on page 69. Sew the blocks together into rows. Join the rows to make the quilt-top center, which should measure 78½" square, including the seam allowances.

2 Join the reserved 2"-wide fabric 6 strips end to end. From the pieced strip, cut two 78½"-long strips and sew them to opposite sides of the quilt top. From the remaining pieced strip, cut two 81½"-long strips and sew them to the top and bottom of the quilt top. Press all seam allowances toward the borders. The quilt top should measure 81½" square, including the seam allowances.

3 Join the brown 2"-wide strips end to end. From the pieced strip, cut two 81½"-long strips and sew them to opposite sides of the quilt top. From the remaining pieced strip, cut two 84½"-long strips and sew them to the top and bottom of the quilt top. Press all seam allowances toward the borders. The quilt top should measure 84½" square.

Finishing the Quilt

For more details on any finishing steps, go to ShopMartingale.com/HowtoQuilt to download free illustrated information.

1 Layer the quilt top with batting and backing; baste. Machine quilt a decorative design across the surface of the quilt (or take the top and backing to a professional long-arm machine quilter).

2 Add a label.

3 Using the dark brown 2¼"-wide strips, make the binding and attach it to the quilt.

Adding a Label

Many people leave the label to the last step, but I prefer to incorporate it into the binding for a secure hold that guards the label against coming loose. I create a label on printable fabric and press a seam allowance on two adjacent edges. Next, I pin the label onto the back of the quilt, aligning the two raw edges with one of the bottom corners. After adding the binding, I hand stitch the other two sides of the label onto the backing.

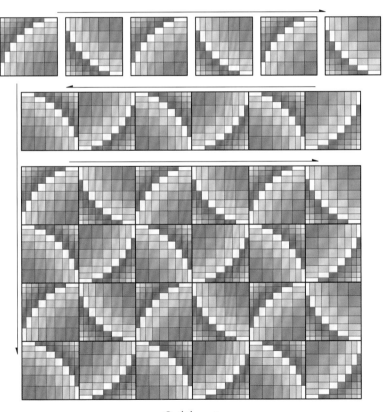

Quilt layout

Stormy Seas

I had the idea in my head to create a design with an X in the middle and "other bits" around it, not being certain what the other parts of the design should be. It took many iterations, but eventually this design emerged. I played around with various colorways until I landed on this one, which just looked right because it brought to mind waves crashing over one another during a storm at sea. So as not to overwhelm myself with the size and weight of the quilt, I designed it with only 16 colors. Even so, it's turned out rather on the large side.

Fabric Selection

Choose 16 fabrics in two color groups: one group of three purple fabrics, and a second group of 13 turquoise fabrics. Each color group should represent a range of values from light to dark.

Materials

Yardage is based on 42"-wide fabric.

1 yard *each* of 15 assorted purple and turquoise fabrics for bargello (fabrics 1–14 and 16)

2⅜ yards of dark teal print for bargello, border, and binding (fabric 15)

9 yards of fabric for backing

108" × 108" piece of batting

Cutting

All measurements include ¼"-wide seam allowances.

From *each* of fabrics 1–14 and 16, cut:
11 strips, 2½" × 42"

From fabric 15, cut:
11 strips, 2½" × 42"
11 strips, 2" × 42"
11 strips, 2¼" × 42"

Preparation

Referring to "Preparing a Fabric Guide" on page 8, assemble a fabric guide using a scrap of each of the 16 fabrics. Arrange them in order from lightest purple (fabric 1) to darkest turquoise (fabric 16). This will ensure the fabrics are in the right order when making the strip sets.

Prepare a set of labels for columns 1–49 (*column 1, column 2,* etc.) to pin on the completed columns.

Making the Strip Sets

Referring to "Sewing Strip Sets" on page 10 and using the 2½"-wide strips, sort the strips into 11 groups, with one strip of each fabric in each group. Arrange the strips in each group in numerical order. Sew the strips in each group together to make 11 strip sets. Press the seam allowances toward fabric 1 on five strip sets and toward fabric 16 on the remaining six strip sets.

Fabric 1		Fabric 1
Fabric 2		Fabric 2
Fabric 3		Fabric 3
Fabric 4		Fabric 4
Fabric 5		Fabric 5
Fabric 6		Fabric 6
Fabric 7		Fabric 7
Fabric 8		Fabric 8
Fabric 9		Fabric 9
Fabric 10		Fabric 10
Fabric 11		Fabric 11
Fabric 12		Fabric 12
Fabric 13		Fabric 13
Fabric 14		Fabric 14
Fabric 15		Fabric 15
Fabric 16		Fabric 16

Make 5.   Make 6.

Making Column 1

Refer to "Cutting Strip Sets" on page 13 for more information as needed.

1 Cut three 1"-wide segments from a strip set with the seam allowances pressed toward fabric 1.

2 Sew fabric 16 on the first segment to fabric 1 on the second segment. Sew fabric 1 on the third segment to fabric 16 on the second segment. Then sew the ends (fabrics 1 and 16) together to make a loop.

3 Turn the loop right side out. Use a seam ripper to remove the stitching between fabrics 8 and 9. Fabric 9 will be at the top of the column. Press all seam allowances toward the top of the column.

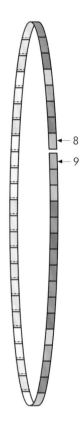

4 Compare your finished column to column 1 of the Stormy Seas design tables on pages 76–79. The numbers assigned to your fabrics should match the numbers in the table, and you should have 48 fabrics in your column. Pin the column 1 label to the top of the finished column.

Making Column 2

1 Cut three 1¼"-wide segments from a strip set with the seam allowances pressed toward fabric 16.

2 On the first segment, use a seam ripper to remove the stitching between fabrics 7 and 8. Reserve the 1–7 piece to use in step 7.

3 On the second segment, use a seam ripper to remove the stitching between fabrics 2 and 3. Reserve the 1–2 piece to use in step 6.

4 Sew fabric 16 on the first segment to fabric 3 on the second segment.

5 On the third segment, sew fabric 1 to fabric 16 to make a loop. Use a seam ripper to remove the stitching between fabrics 14 and 15. Sew fabric 16 on the second segment to fabric 15 on the third segment. Fabric 14 will be at the bottom of the column.

6 Sew fabric 1 on the two-fabric piece from step 3 to fabric 14 at the bottom of the column. Fabric 2 will now be at the bottom of the column.

7 Sew fabric 1 on the 1–7 piece from step 2 to fabric 2 at the bottom of the column. Press all seam allowances toward the bottom of the column.

8 Compare your finished column to column 2 of the design table. The numbers assigned to your fabrics should match the numbers in the table, and you should have 48 fabrics in your column. Pin the column 2 label to the top of the finished column.

Making Column 3

1 Cut three 1½"-wide segments from a strip set with the seam allowances pressed toward fabric 1.

2 On the first segment, use a seam ripper to remove the stitching between fabrics 6 and 7. Reserve the 1–6 piece to use in step 7.

3 On the second segment, use a seam ripper to remove the stitching between fabrics 4 and 5. Reserve the 1–4 piece to use in step 6.

4 Sew fabric 16 on the first segment to fabric 5 on the second segment.

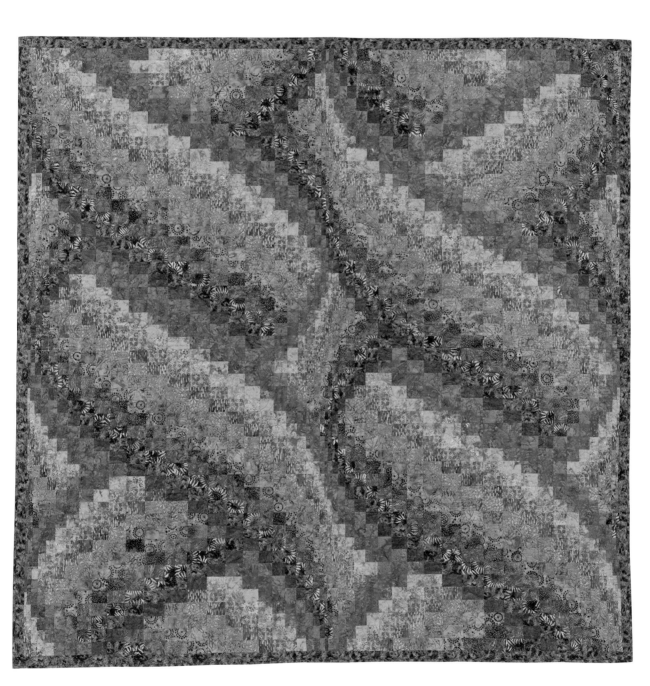

FINISHED SIZE: 100" × 99½"
Pieced by Judith Steele; quilted by Trish Ryan.

5 On the third segment, sew fabric 1 to fabric 16 to make a loop. Use a seam ripper to remove the stitching between fabrics 12 and 13. Sew fabric 16 on the second segment to fabric 13 on the third segment. Fabric 12 will be at the bottom of the column.

6 Sew fabric 1 on the 1–4 piece from step 3 to fabric 12 at the bottom of the column. Fabric 4 will now be at the bottom of the column.

7 Sew fabric 1 on the 1–6 piece from step 2 to fabric 4 at the bottom of the column. Press all seam allowances toward the top of the column.

8 Compare your finished column to column 3 of the design table. The numbers assigned to your fabrics should match the numbers in the table, and you should have 48 fabrics in your column. Pin the column 3 label to the top of the finished column.

Working from the Design Table

1 Continue working in the same manner, cutting three segments each for columns 4–9, 17, 25, 33, and 41–49 in the widths indicated in the design tables on pages 76–79. Cut four segments each for columns 10–16, 18–24, 26–32, and 34–40 in the widths indicated. After column 14, you may be able to use some of the reserved segments from previous columns to help you complete the additional columns. (Leftover segments that are too wide can be cut down to the required size.) Referring to your fabric guide and using the bold lines on the design tables as a reference, remove the stitching between fabrics, as needed, and join the segments in the order indicated for the column you are making.

2 After completing each new column, compare it to the design table to make sure the fabric numbers and pressing direction are accurate. Then pin the appropriate label to the top of the column.

Assembling the Quilt Top

1 With right sides together and starting with columns 1 and 2, join the columns in pairs, sewing along their long edges and carefully matching the seam intersections. Press the seam allowances toward the odd-numbered columns.

2 Join the pairs and press the seam allowances toward the lower-numbered columns.

3 Continue in this manner until all the columns have been joined. The quilt-top center should measure 97" × 96½", including the seam allowances.

4 Join the dark teal 2"-wide strips end to end. From the pieced strip, cut two 96½"-long strips and sew them to the sides of the quilt top. From the remaining pieced strip, cut two 100"-long strips and sew them to the top and bottom of the quilt top. Press all seam allowances toward the dark teal strips. The quilt top should measure 100" × 99½".

Finishing the Quilt

For more details on any finishing steps, go to ShopMartingale.com/HowtoQuilt to download free illustrated information.

1 Layer the quilt top with batting and backing; baste. Machine quilt a decorative design across the surface of the quilt (or take the top and backing to a professional long-arm machine quilter).

2 Add a label.

3 Using the dark teal 2¼"-wide strips, make the binding and attach it to the quilt.

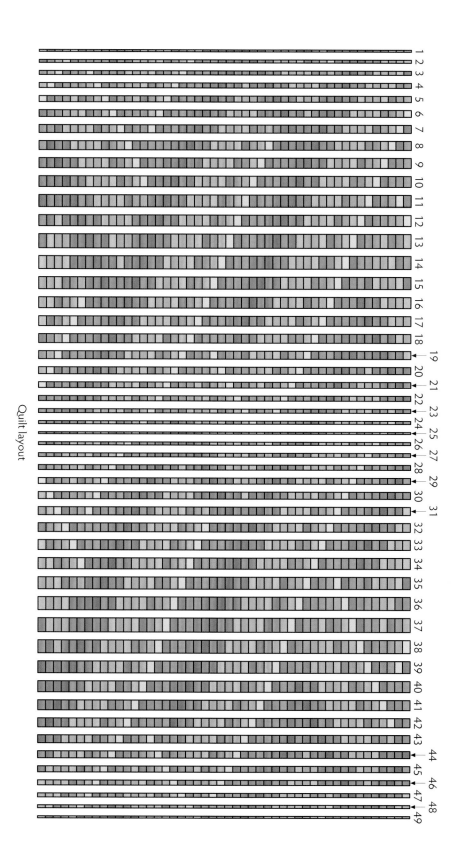

Quilt layout

Design Table: Stormy Seas

SECTION 1														
Column	1	2	3	4	5	6	7	8	9	10	11	12	13	14
Cut width of segments	1"	1¼"	1½"	1¾"	2"	2¼"	2½"	2¾"	3"	3¼"	3½"	3¾"	4"	3¾"
Pressing direction	↑	↓	↑	↓	↑	↓	↑	↓	↑	↓	↑	↓	↑	↓
Number of segments to cut	3	3	3	3	3	3	3	3	3	4	4	4	4	4
Fabric number	9	8	7	6	5	4	3	2	1	2	3	4	5	6
	10	9	8	7	6	5	4	3	2	1	4	5	6	7
	11	10	9	8	7	6	5	4	3	2	1	6	7	8
	12	11	10	9	8	7	6	5	4	3	2	1	8	9
	13	12	11	10	9	8	7	6	5	4	3	2	1	10
	14	13	12	11	10	9	8	7	6	5	4	3	2	1
	15	14	13	12	11	10	9	8	7	6	5	4	3	2
	16	15	14	13	12	11	10	9	8	7	6	5	4	3
	1	16	15	14	13	12	11	10	9	8	7	6	5	4
	2	3	16	15	14	13	12	11	10	9	8	7	6	5
	3	4	5	16	15	14	13	12	11	10	9	8	7	6
	4	5	6	7	16	15	14	13	12	11	10	9	8	7
	5	6	7	8	9	16	15	14	13	12	11	10	9	8
	6	7	8	9	10	11	16	15	14	13	12	11	10	9
	7	8	9	10	11	12	13	16	15	14	13	12	11	10
	8	9	10	11	12	13	14	15	16	15	14	13	12	11
	9	10	11	12	13	14	15	16	1	16	15	14	13	12
	10	11	12	13	14	15	16	3	2	1	16	15	14	13
	11	12	13	14	15	16	5	4	3	2	1	16	15	14
	12	13	14	15	16	7	6	5	4	3	2	1	16	15
	13	14	15	16	9	8	7	6	5	4	3	2	1	16
	14	15	16	11	10	9	8	7	6	5	4	3	2	1
	15	16	13	12	11	10	9	8	7	6	5	4	3	2
	16	15	14	13	12	11	10	9	8	7	6	5	4	3
	1	16	15	14	13	12	11	10	9	8	7	6	5	4
	2	1	16	15	14	13	12	11	10	9	8	7	6	5
	3	2	1	16	15	14	13	12	11	10	9	8	7	6
	4	3	2	1	16	15	14	13	12	11	10	9	8	7
	5	4	3	2	1	16	15	14	13	12	11	10	9	8
	6	5	4	3	2	1	16	15	14	13	12	11	10	9
	7	6	5	4	3	2	1	16	15	14	13	12	11	10
	8	7	6	5	4	3	2	1	16	15	14	13	12	11
	9	8	7	6	5	4	3	2	1	16	15	14	13	12
	10	9	8	7	6	5	4	1	2	3	16	15	14	13
	11	10	9	8	7	6	1	2	3	4	5	16	15	14
	12	11	10	9	8	1	2	3	4	5	6	7	16	15
	13	12	11	10	1	2	3	4	5	6	7	8	9	16
	14	13	12	1	2	3	4	5	6	7	8	9	10	11
	15	14	1	2	3	4	5	6	7	8	9	10	11	12

Attach to top of Section 1 on page 79.

strip-pieced bargello

SECTION 2

Column	15	16	17	18	19	20	21	22	23	24	25	26	27	28	29	30
Cut width of segments	3½"	3¼"	3"	2¾"	2½"	2¼"	2"	1¾"	1½"	1¼"	1"	1¼"	1½"	1¾"	2"	2¼"
Pressing direction	↑	↓	↑	↓	↑	↓	↑	↓	↑	↓	↑	↓	↑	↓	↑	↓
Number of segments to cut	4	4	3	4	4	4	4	4	4	4	3	4	4	4	4	4
Fabric number	7	8	9	10	11	12	13	14	15	16	1	16	15	14	13	12
	8	9	10	11	12	13	14	15	16	3	2	1	16	15	14	13
	9	10	11	12	13	14	15	16	5	4	3	2	1	16	15	14
	10	11	12	13	14	15	16	7	6	5	4	3	2	1	16	15
	11	12	13	14	15	16	9	8	7	6	5	4	3	2	1	16
	12	13	14	15	16	11	10	9	8	7	6	5	4	3	2	1
	1	14	15	16	13	12	11	10	9	8	7	6	5	4	3	2
	2	1	16	15	14	13	12	11	10	9	8	7	6	5	4	3
	3	2	1	16	15	14	13	12	11	10	9	8	7	6	5	4
	4	3	2	1	16	15	14	13	12	11	10	9	8	7	6	5
	5	4	3	2	1	16	15	14	13	12	11	10	9	8	7	6
	6	5	4	3	2	1	16	15	14	13	12	11	10	9	8	7
	7	6	5	4	3	2	1	16	15	14	13	12	11	10	9	8
	8	7	6	5	4	3	2	1	16	15	14	13	12	11	10	9
	9	8	7	6	5	4	3	2	1	16	15	14	13	12	11	10
	10	9	8	7	6	5	4	3	2	1	16	15	14	13	12	11
	11	10	9	8	7	6	5	4	3	2	1	16	15	14	13	12
	12	11	10	9	8	7	6	5	4	1	2	3	16	15	14	13
	13	12	11	10	9	8	7	6	1	2	3	4	5	16	15	14
	14	13	12	11	10	9	8	1	2	3	4	5	6	7	16	15
	15	14	13	12	11	10	1	2	3	4	5	6	7	8	9	16
	16	15	14	13	12	1	2	3	4	5	6	7	8	9	10	11
	1	16	15	14	1	2	3	4	5	6	7	8	9	10	11	12
	2	1	16	1	2	3	4	5	6	7	8	9	10	11	12	13
	3	2	1	2	3	4	5	6	7	8	9	10	11	12	13	14
	4	3	2	1	4	5	6	7	8	9	10	11	12	13	14	15
	5	4	3	2	1	6	7	8	9	10	11	12	13	14	15	16
	6	5	4	3	2	1	8	9	10	11	12	13	14	15	16	7
	7	6	5	4	3	2	1	10	11	12	13	14	15	16	9	8
	8	7	6	5	4	3	2	1	12	13	14	15	16	11	10	9
	9	8	7	6	5	4	3	2	1	14	15	16	13	12	11	10
	10	9	8	7	6	5	4	3	2	1	16	15	14	13	12	11
	11	10	9	8	7	6	5	4	3	2	1	16	15	14	13	12
	12	11	10	9	8	7	6	5	4	3	2	1	16	15	14	13
	13	12	11	10	9	8	7	6	5	4	3	2	1	16	15	14
	14	13	12	11	10	9	8	7	6	5	4	3	2	1	16	15
	15	14	13	12	11	10	9	8	7	6	5	4	3	2	1	16
	16	15	14	13	12	11	10	9	8	7	6	5	4	3	2	1
	13	16	15	14	13	12	11	10	9	8	7	6	5	4	3	2

Attach to top of Section 2 on page 79.

Column	31	32	33	34	35	36	37	38	39	40	41	42	43	44	45	46	47	48	49
Cut width of segments	2½"	2¾"	3"	3¼"	3½"	3¾"	4"	3¾"	3½"	3¼"	3"	2¾"	2½"	2¼"	2"	1¾"	1½"	1¼"	1"
Pressing direction	↑	↓	↑	↓	↑	↓	↑	↓	↑	↓	↑	↓	↑	↓	↑	↓	↑	↓	↑
Number of segments to cut	4	4	3	4	4	4	4	4	4	4	3	3	3	3	3	3	3	3	3
Fabric number	11	10	9	8	7	6	5	4	3	2	1	16	15	14	13	12	11	10	9
	12	11	10	9	8	7	6	5	4	1	2	3	16	15	14	13	12	11	10
	13	12	11	10	9	8	7	6	1	2	3	4	5	16	15	14	13	12	11
	14	13	12	11	10	9	8	1	2	3	4	5	6	7	16	15	14	13	12
	15	14	13	12	11	10	1	2	3	4	5	6	7	8	9	16	15	14	13
	16	15	14	13	12	1	2	3	4	5	6	7	8	9	10	11	16	15	14
	1	16	15	14	1	2	3	4	5	6	7	8	9	10	11	12	13	16	15
	2	1	16	1	2	3	4	5	6	7	8	9	10	11	12	13	14	15	16
	3	2	1	2	3	4	5	6	7	8	9	10	11	12	13	14	15	16	1
	4	3	2	1	4	5	6	7	8	9	10	11	12	13	14	15	16	3	2
	5	4	3	2	1	6	7	8	9	10	11	12	13	14	15	16	5	4	3
	6	5	4	3	2	1	8	9	10	11	12	13	14	15	16	7	6	5	4
	7	6	5	4	3	2	1	10	11	12	13	14	15	16	9	8	7	6	5
	8	7	6	5	4	3	2	1	12	13	14	15	16	11	10	9	8	7	6
	9	8	7	6	5	4	3	2	1	14	15	16	13	12	11	10	9	8	7
	10	9	8	7	6	5	4	3	2	1	16	15	14	13	12	11	10	9	8
	11	10	9	8	7	6	5	4	3	2	1	16	15	14	13	12	11	10	9
	12	11	10	9	8	7	6	5	4	3	2	1	16	15	14	13	12	11	10
	13	12	11	10	9	8	7	6	5	4	3	2	1	16	15	14	13	12	11
	14	13	12	11	10	9	8	7	6	5	4	3	2	1	16	15	14	13	12
	15	14	13	12	11	10	9	8	7	6	5	4	3	2	1	16	15	14	13
	16	15	14	13	12	11	10	9	8	7	6	5	4	3	2	1	16	15	14
	13	16	15	14	13	12	11	10	9	8	7	6	5	4	3	2	1	16	15
	14	15	16	15	14	13	12	11	10	9	8	7	6	5	4	3	2	1	16
	15	16	1	16	15	14	13	12	11	10	9	8	7	6	5	4	3	2	1
	16	3	2	1	16	15	14	13	12	11	10	9	8	7	6	5	4	1	2
	5	4	3	2	1	16	15	14	13	12	11	10	9	8	7	6	1	2	3
	6	5	4	3	2	1	16	15	14	13	12	11	10	9	8	1	2	3	4
	7	6	5	4	3	2	1	16	15	14	13	12	11	10	1	2	3	4	5
	8	7	6	5	4	3	2	1	16	15	14	13	12	1	2	3	4	5	6
	9	8	7	6	5	4	3	2	1	16	15	14	1	2	3	4	5	6	7
	10	9	8	7	6	5	4	3	2	1	16	1	2	3	4	5	6	7	8
	11	10	9	8	7	6	5	4	3	2	1	2	3	4	5	6	7	8	9
	12	11	10	9	8	7	6	5	4	3	2	1	4	5	6	7	8	9	10
	13	12	11	10	9	8	7	6	5	4	3	2	1	6	7	8	9	10	11
	14	13	12	11	10	9	8	7	6	5	4	3	2	1	8	9	10	11	12
	15	14	13	12	11	10	9	8	7	6	5	4	3	2	1	10	11	12	13
	16	15	14	13	12	11	10	9	8	7	6	5	4	3	2	1	12	13	14
	1	16	15	14	13	12	11	10	9	8	7	6	5	4	3	2	1	14	15

Attach to top of Section 3 on page 79.

Attach to bottom of Section 1 on page 76.

SECTION 1

Column	1	2	3	4	5	6	7	8	9	10	11	12	13	14
Fabric number	16	1	2	3	4	5	6	7	8	9	10	11	12	13
	1	2	3	4	5	6	7	8	9	10	11	12	13	14
	2	1	4	5	6	7	8	9	10	11	12	13	14	15
	3	2	1	6	7	8	9	10	11	12	13	14	15	16
	4	3	2	1	8	9	10	11	12	13	14	15	16	7
	5	4	3	2	1	10	11	12	13	14	15	16	9	8
	6	5	4	3	2	1	12	13	14	15	16	11	10	9
	7	6	5	4	3	2	1	14	15	16	13	12	11	10
	8	7	6	5	4	3	2	1	16	15	14	13	12	11

Attach to bottom of Section 2 on page 77.

SECTION 2

Column	15	16	17	18	19	20	21	22	23	24	25	26	27	28	29	30
Fabric number	14	15	16	15	14	13	12	11	10	9	8	7	6	5	4	3
	15	16	1	16	15	14	13	12	11	10	9	8	7	6	5	4
	16	3	2	1	16	15	14	13	12	11	10	9	8	7	6	5
	5	4	3	2	1	16	15	14	13	12	11	10	9	8	7	6
	6	5	4	3	2	1	16	15	14	13	12	11	10	9	8	1
	7	6	5	4	3	2	1	16	15	14	13	12	11	10	1	2
	8	7	6	5	4	3	2	1	16	15	14	13	12	1	2	3
	9	8	7	6	5	4	3	2	1	16	15	14	1	2	3	4
	10	9	8	7	6	5	4	3	2	1	16	1	2	3	4	5

Attach to bottom of Section 3 on page 78.

SECTION 3

Column	31	32	33	34	35	36	37	38	39	40	41	42	43	44	45	46	47	48	49
Fabric number	2	1	16	15	14	13	12	11	10	9	8	7	6	5	4	3	2	1	16
	3	2	1	16	15	14	13	12	11	10	9	8	7	6	5	4	3	2	1
	4	1	2	3	16	15	14	13	12	11	10	9	8	7	6	5	4	3	2
	1	2	3	4	5	16	15	14	13	12	11	10	9	8	7	6	5	4	3
	2	3	4	5	6	7	16	15	14	13	12	11	10	9	8	7	6	5	4
	3	4	5	6	7	8	9	16	15	14	13	12	11	10	9	8	7	6	5
	4	5	6	7	8	9	10	11	16	15	14	13	12	11	10	9	8	7	6
	5	6	7	8	9	10	11	12	13	16	15	14	13	12	11	10	9	8	7
	6	7	8	9	10	11	12	13	14	15	16	15	14	13	12	11	10	9	8

About the Author

Growing up in a small country town located in the central highlands of the state of Victoria in southeastern Australia, an accepted part of Judith Steele's early life was that you sewed and knitted. Her mother pursued these activities while her father fed Judith's interest in all things precise and technical, running a small engineering business from the large shed next to the house. She loved spending time surrounded by the smell of engine oil while watching metal shavings curl off the items he machined on his lathes.

Judith learned to knit at the age of four, although nothing useful appeared for many years. Her first sewing project was a dress of dark blue and orange, leading to many other dressmaking projects that included her wedding dress and many children's clothes.

Following a career in carpet designing, a bumpy married life, and three children, Judith became captivated by computing. In 1992 she achieved the degree of Bachelor of Computing at La Trobe University in Bendigo, Victoria. Several years of teaching and working as a support analyst eventually led her to move to the state of Western Australia, where she worked for the state government while pursuing her passion for patchwork and quilting.

Judith was bitten by the quilting bug in 1999. After winning a copy of Electric Quilt, she found that designing became much easier, and a number of her bargello designs have been published in various Australian quilting magazines. Bargello quilts are her primary love, but she relishes experimenting with anything that she can design using EQ8 on her computer.

Acknowledgments

First, I'd like to acknowledge that the inspiration for all the projects in this book came from God, my Heavenly Father. Without Him, none of this would have happened.

The earthly people who have provided the most ongoing support and encouragement are the members of my Wednesday sewing group: Trish, Maureen, Lynne, and Daphne. These wonderful ladies have provided the impetus I needed to stay on track, especially when I felt low and unmotivated.

Other groups that have provided motivation and stimulus are the ladies from the Foothills Friendship Quilters, the Western Australian Quilters Association, and my friends at Southern River Church of Christ.

Thank you to everyone.